"Hearing the voice of God doesn't have to be arduous or difficult. Jesus made it quite evident that His sheep know His voice. Steve Sampson has been one of those precious Kingdom treasures whom God has used to equip and empower His people to recognize and obey His voice. With clarity and humor, Steve takes you on a journey to the place of profound simplicity in Christ where hearing Him is as natural as breathing in the air that sustains you. I am delighted that he has revised, updated and expanded his classic work *You Can Hear the Voice of God*. Let Steve take you step by step, progressively and with grace, into a reawakening and renewing of the presence and the promptings of the Spirit in your life."

Bishop Mark J. Chironna, M.A., Ph.D.,
Church on the Living Edge, Orlando, Florida

"It is my pleasure to recommend Steve Sampson's book *You Can Hear the Voice of God*. If I had not read the book, I could still recommend it because its very title causes me to say to you, 'I heard Steve Sampson's voice, and I know the quality of what he is going to say is consistent with his life.' Thank you for the privilege of participating in the ministry of my friend."

Dr. Robert Cornwall, traveling minister

YOU CAN
HEAR THE
VOICE
OF GOD

Other Books by Steve Sampson

Breaking the Bondage Barrier . . . Taking the Limits Off God

*Confronting Jezebel: Discerning and
Defeating the Spirit of Control*

*Discerning and Defeating the Ahab Spirit:
The Key to Breaking Free from Jezebel*

Don't Talk to Me Now, Lord . . . I'm Trying to Pray

I Was Always on My Mind

Those Who Expect Nothing Are Never Disappointed

You Can Hear the Voice of God

You Can't Use Me Today, Lord . . . I Don't Feel Spiritual

REVISED AND EXPANDED EDITION

YOU CAN HEAR THE VOICE OF GOD

HOW GOD SPEAKS IN LISTENING PRAYER

STEVE SAMPSON

Chosen

a division of Baker Publishing Group
Minneapolis, Minnesota

Original edition published by Sovereign World Limited of Tonbridge Kent, England

Published by Chosen Books
11400 Hampshire Avenue South
Bloomington, Minnesota 55438
www.chosenbooks.com

Chosen Books is a division of
Baker Publishing Group, Grand Rapids, Michigan

Printed in the United States of America

Library of Congress Cataloging-in-Publication Data
Sampson, Steve.
    You can hear the voice of God : how God speaks in listening prayer / Steve Sampson. — Revised and Expanded Edition.
        pages cm
    Summary: "Uncomplicated, unique, and incredibly practical, this book prepares readers to enjoy two-way conversation with God; now revised and expanded with even more real-life instruction" —Provided by publisher.
    ISBN 978-0-8007-9614-3 (pbk. : alk. paper)
    1. Spiritual life—Christianity. 2. Hearing—Religious aspects—Christianity.
I. Title.
BV 4509.5.S25 2015
248.4—dc23   2014041709

The names and other identifying details of certain individuals have been changed to protect their privacy.

Cover design by Gearbox

15 16 17 18 19 20 21   7 6 5 4 3 2 1

Contents

Introduction

Learning to Know His Voice

Part of me wanted to title this book *Ten Ways to Hear from God*, because through my years of personal experience, I have recognized at least ten ways that the Holy Spirit speaks to us. My thinking was that in reading these pages, you might reason, *I may not be able to hear God in all ten ways, but maybe I can hear Him in at least one or two.* Listening for God in a couple of ways is certainly better than not expecting to hear from Him at all, but it is still too limiting. I am confident, however, that if you will apply the simple principles I present in these pages, you will hear Him in many ways.

In this new and revised edition, I will be sharing firsthand illustrations of my own experiences over the years. This book is easy to read, and the principles are simple, yet profound. They have proven true repeatedly in my experience for over thirty years. I have been blessed with so much positive feedback from those who have related how these truths have changed their lives and enabled them to begin hearing the Holy Spirit—daily.

Henry Ford had an amazing vision. He wanted every person to be able to own an automobile. Toward that end, his company manufactured millions of affordable Model T and Model A Fords. My vision is similar—that every Christian be able to hear the voice of the Lord.

If you have an earnest desire to hear from God, this book will be life-changing for you. Jesus said, "My sheep hear My voice" (John 10:27). He did not say certain sheep or special sheep. *You* can hear His voice. Yet hearing Him is not just about prayer, but about listening when we pray. Hearing the voice of God should be the most basic, foundational thing we learn as new Christians. Little is written on the subject, however, at least in any practical sense. Learning to hear is a process. Just as a child learns to talk and walk, we all grow in our confidence when it comes to hearing God. The key is not to let religious activity become a substitute for intimacy with God.

This book is not a work to convince the skeptics, but rather to feed and equip the hungry. I am in no way trying to be a theologian, but rather, I am sharing with you the principles the Lord has taught me (combined with experience). This entire book gives practical instruction on how to stir up the Holy Spirit and begin to hear His voice daily. Christians are weary of fleshly hype and hoopla; they desire to hear the Master's voice. There is a divine desire kindled afresh in the hearts of believers everywhere to know the mind of the Spirit and to expend energy only on that to which He has called them. Hearing God is encountering life. Yes, it is possible to hear from Him—daily.

As a pastor, I noticed firsthand something about those who were growing spiritually. They would always relate how they had heard the Holy Spirit speak to them through a Scripture, or in some other way, that made them aware that they were communicating with Him. As a result, their spiritual growth was phenomenal, while the growth of others seemed stunted. Hearing God's voice has a huge impact on your growth rate as a Christian.

At first, it seems easy to grow. New converts always seem to have wonderful experiences in the first days of their Christian experience. They may not have a lot of wisdom, but their receptivity and response to the Holy Spirit is precious and priceless. They may not know Genesis from Revelation, but they have an amazing awareness of the Holy Spirit talking to them.

As weeks turn into months, however, new believers generally experience hearing the Lord's voice less and less. Distractions begin to take over. Sincere Christian leaders involve baby Christians in church activities and quickly give them a job title, involving them in special projects and immersing them in all manner of religious busyness. Yet nothing is done to train those spiritual babies to exercise their spirits by listening to the Lord. All the emphasis is placed on looking *outside,* not *inside.* The spiritual growth of new believers stops because communion with the Holy Spirit stops. Instead, they are taught to trust a prominent Christian magazine, the denominational headquarters or a popular and gifted teacher rather than trusting the Holy Spirit within. The simple truth has been forgotten, the most basic New Covenant principle, "None of them shall teach his neighbor, and none his brother, saying, 'Know the LORD,' for all shall know Me, from the least of them to the greatest of them" (Hebrews 8:11).

Frankly, I believe Christians do hear God; they just have not been taught to recognize His voice. All manner of things have clogged our ears. The devil has issued a universal assignment to obstruct our hearing, because he knows that Christians who are in intimate communion with the Holy Spirit are a serious threat to his kingdom. Those who hear God are capable of *knowing* the mind of the Spirit and receiving strategies in prayer—strategies that will expose the enemy's tactics.

Yet we cannot solely blame the devil, for it is really the lack of proper direction that has robbed us. We have substituted religious gobbledygook for training our young believers' spirits to be resilient in hearing the Lord. Even the writer of Hebrews laments "you have *become dull of hearing*" (Hebrews 5:11, emphasis added). The implication is that we were born with good spiritual ears, but we have not trained and disciplined ourselves to pay attention to the Holy Spirit, thus we have become dull of hearing.

Although we may grow in our knowledge of the Word, our spiritual man does not necessarily grow. Information about the Bible does not guarantee revelation of the Spirit. Yet you and I can learn to hear His voice in so many ways. There is nothing more exciting than hearing the Holy Spirit, so get ready for the adventure of your life! Yes, you can hear the voice of God.

Steve Sampson

1

Hearing God through the Written Word and the Proceeding Word

> Man shall not live by bread alone; but man lives by every word that proceeds from the mouth of the LORD.
>
> Deuteronomy 8:3

Pastor Michael was on a weekend ministry trip in the Carolinas. Traveling with him was his music minister, Jason. They both had been looking forward to a weekend of ministering to an excited and expectant group of people. They began Friday night and ministered all day Saturday; then they agreed to stop for a little refreshment before the Saturday night meeting. As they walked into a famous fast-food establishment, Michael ordered a shake. Jason liked the idea and ordered one, too. Unfortuntately, in the thirty-minute drive back to the church, they both began complaining of nausea.

They pulled into the church parking lot just minutes before the meeting began. After several worship songs, Michael was introduced. As he began to preach, his horrible feelings of nausea increased. He prayed under his breath that he would not get violently sick in front of everyone.

Strangely, in the middle of his struggle he sensed the Lord drawing his attention to a young lady on the worship team. Unable to ignore the urging from the Holy Spirit, he heard himself saying to her, "The Lord is telling me that He sees you as pure and innocent, and what you have been through will be as if it never happened."

Michelle, whom he had never met, began to cry loudly. Her mother, who was on the back row of the church, began to wail. Pastor Michael prayed for a few other people and closed the meeting. He felt so sick by then that he turned down the church pastor's invitation to get something to eat afterward. He and Jason went to their motel, where they both vomited excessively. They drew the obvious conclusion that they were suffering from food poisoning.

The following morning, they returned to the church. The pastor could not wait to tell Michael about the effect of the word he had spoken the night before on nineteen-year-old Michelle. Her story was tragic. A few months earlier she had met a man on the Internet, and they had agreed to meet in her small North Carolina town. On a date, he had drugged her soft drink and brutally raped her. Her sister found her naked body on the front porch the following morning.

A few days before the ministry weekend, Michelle had finally gotten up the courage to tell her mother about the entire horrendous experience. Her mother was reeling from grief. Then right before the Saturday night meeting, Michelle told her mother that this would be her last church service because she just could not deal with the guilt and shame of her rape. The only reason she agreed to go to the meeting that summer night was that the music team desperately needed her help, but Michelle had already determined that this would be her last appearance in church.

When I heard the story, I marveled at the ministry of the Holy Spirit. Michelle had reached her end, but God spoke through Pastor Michael to bring her a message of hope and healing. The prophetic word to Michelle—that God saw her as clean and innocent—liberated her from the devastating shame and guilt that made her want to surrender to a life of hopelessness. The change in her life was immediate.

The story made me think of how deviously the powers of darkness had strategized to make Pastor Michael so sick that he would become ineffective. This was not unlike the severe storm that the disciples encountered when crossing the Sea of Galilee, just before Jesus cast the demons out of the man living in the cemetery of the Gadarenes (see Luke 8).

It made me wonder how many desperate people attend church, despairing over a situation and needing to hear God speak to them, but then leave the meeting just as they came—empty and discouraged.

The Proceeding Word

Michael's experience of giving that word to Michelle is a perfect illustration of a powerful truth in Scripture—the need to hear the proceeding Word of God. Scripture tells us,

> And you shall remember that the LORD your God led you all the way these forty years in the wilderness, to humble you and test you, to know what was in your heart, whether you would keep His commandments or not. So He humbled you,

allowed you to hunger, and fed you with manna which you did not know nor did your fathers know, that He might make you know that man shall not live by bread alone; *but man lives by every word that proceeds from the mouth of the* LORD.

Deuteronomy 8:2–3 (emphasis added)

The truth is that God wants to speak to all His people, and even more important, He wants to speak *through* all His people. Michelle needed to hear more than a sermon. She needed to hear a personal word from the Holy Spirit that would release her from her deplorable encounter. Thankfully, Pastor Michael was available for the Lord to speak through that summer night.

There is no question that God speaks to us through the written Word (the *logos*), which is the established mind of God and the will of God. It is one thing, however, to know what God has said in His Word, but it is also another thing of great significance to know what the Holy Spirit is saying to us daily through the proceeding word.

Think of it this way: The Bible is our road map, while the Holy Spirit is our transportation. Growing up in an evangelical church, I cannot tell you how many times I heard entire sermons on the importance of the written Word of God, and statements such as, "All we need is the Word." Personally, the only time I heard the Holy Spirit mentioned was at water baptism, when the preacher would say, "In the name of the Father, the Son and the Holy Spirit." Some evangelicals claim that the gifts of the Holy Spirit are not for our day and time, but ended when the apostles and disciples died. They say that God does not speak today other than through His Word, and they seem to view the Trinity as the Father, the Son and the Holy Bible.

This attitude makes my blood boil. As we read and study the Bible, it tells us that God is willing to speak to us in a variety of ways and will give us personal instruction and guidance in everything that concerns our lives. The Bible is full of miracles and demonstrations of the active power of the Holy Spirit. The book of Acts is a great example of that. It is amazing how many times the disciples had to listen to direction from the Holy Spirit in that book.

The Bible instructs us to be led by the Holy Spirit (see Romans 8:14). Jesus said, "My sheep hear My voice" (John 10:27). Multiple Scriptures tell us to listen to and obey God. But how can we obey God if we never hear Him? Do we just read the Word, or do we start believing it and acting on what it says?

Most everyone can relate experiences of how they have merely opened the Bible and had a verse of Scripture seemingly jump off the page at them. Those experiences, of which God has graciously given me many, are priceless. The Bible is what some call the "Manufacturer's Handbook." As Peter states, "All Scripture is given by inspiration of God, and is profitable for doctrine, for reproof, for correction, for instruction in righteousness, that the man of God may be complete, thoroughly equipped for every good work" (2 Timothy 3:16–17). Yet it is one thing to read a book and quite another to know the author. Until the Author, the Holy Spirit, makes the Word come alive, it is only ink on paper. Without the help of the Holy Spirit, we will not experience the flow of life that comes through the written Word.

Again, the best way I find to express this is that the Bible is our road map, but the Holy Spirit is our transportation. I thank God for the Bible; it is our map and our pathway to life. But it is one thing to have a road map, or a GPS system, and another thing to have a car to drive. What good is a GPS without transportation? A GPS will give us directions, but ultimately we have to get in a car and drive.

Romans 8:14 says, "For as many as are led by the Spirit of God, these are sons of God." Sometimes when I read the Bible, it helps me to read what it *does not* say. Notice it does not say, "as many as are led by their Bibles." It says "led by the Spirit of God." It also does not say, "Trust in the LORD with all your brain" in Proverbs 3:5; it says "Trust in the LORD with all your heart." Every Christian should study, memorize and absorb the words of Scripture, but we must also have a relationship with the Holy Spirit. Again, man shall not live by bread alone, but by every word that proceeds from the mouth of God. We need the written Word, but we also need the proceeding word, which comes out of our relationship with the Holy Spirit.

The early Christians did not have the luxury of a New Testament to read, but they did hear the Holy Spirit. For example, look at how the Holy Spirit directed Paul, Silas and Timothy:

> Now when they had gone through Phrygia and the region of Galatia, they were *forbidden by the Holy Spirit* to preach the word in Asia. After they had come to Mysia, they tried to go into Bithynia, *but the Spirit did not permit them.* So passing by Mysia, they came down to Troas. And *a vision appeared to Paul in the night.* A man of Macedonia stood and pleaded with him, saying, "Come over to Macedonia and help us." *Now after he had seen the vision, immediately we sought to go to Macedonia, concluding that the Lord had called us to preach the gospel to them.*
>
> Acts 16:6–10, emphasis added

Forbidden by the Holy Spirit? How did they know the Holy Spirit was forbidding them to preach in Asia? I thought it was always God's will to preach anywhere.

The Spirit did not permit them? How did they know that the Holy Spirit was not permitting them to go to Bithynia?

A vision appeared to Paul in the night? How did they know that meant they were to preach in Macedonia?

The answer to these questions is that they were hearing the voice of God.

You Did Not Believe My Words. . . .

Zacharias and Elizabeth were wonderful, God-fearing people with a flawless reputation. Luke 1:6 says, "And they were both righteous before God, walking in all the commandments and ordinances of the Lord blameless." But when the angel Gabriel appeared to Zacharias, he had trouble believing the angel's words.

Gabriel told Zacharias, "Do not be afraid, Zacharias, for your prayer is heard; and your wife Elizabeth will bear you a son, and you shall call his name John" (verse 13).

Zacharias questioned the proclamation, which was a proceeding word from God. He said to the angel, "How shall I know this? For I am an old man, and my wife is well advanced in years" (verse 18). (We know we are in trouble when we are trying to give God "unknown information.")

Gabriel was not happy with Zacharias's response and made it clear that he had been sent from God Himself with the message. Then he said, "But behold, you will be mute and not able to speak until the day these things take place, because you did not believe my words which will be fulfilled in their own time" (verse 20).

Notice the angel did not say, "because you did not believe the Bible." He said, "because you did not believe my words." We can easily be guilty of the same kind of disbelief. Of course we would never reject the Bible . . . but we ignore the Holy Spirit when He speaks to us. The Bible is full of places where the Holy Spirit gives commands, and God still gives us commands today through His Spirit. We need to keep in mind John 15:14: "You are My friends if you do whatever I command you."

God Thinks He Is Right

Keith was the pastor of a small church in a sleepy town in the southern United States. He and his wife had worked hard getting the church off the ground for several years—their biggest struggle being with religious strongholds in the area. By this, I mean people who were self-sufficient and satisfied in their Christian or "religious" experience.

Every week for several years, Pastor Keith and his wife prayed for breakthrough over spiritual blindness and broke the powers of spiritual darkness over their town, knowing that this was where God had called them. One afternoon, Pastor Keith walked into the church and noticed someone had left a message on the church's voicemail. It was a man named Jerry. Jerry expressed that although he and his wife, Jackie, had driven by the church many times, they had never attended a meeting. On voicemail, he left a prayer request regarding Jackie. She had had a stroke a few days earlier and had totally lost her sight. Jerry related that the neurosurgeon had told him that if Jackie was blind for more than 48 hours, her sight would never return.

As Pastor Keith listened to the message, he had a strong prompting from the Holy Spirit to call Jerry. When he dialed the number, however, Jackie answered. Pastor Keith told her that he had received her husband's message about her blindness, and that as he was listening to the voicemail, the Holy Spirit had spoken to him. He was to give her the message that he was hearing in his spirit—the Lord was saying that she would have her eyesight back in two weeks.

Pastor Keith struggled for a way to explain to Jackie what was going on, thinking she might hang up on him. But to his amazement, Jackie's comments in reply were full of faith.

At one point, Jackie told him, "Oh, then I won't have to wear my Stevie Wonder glasses."

Pastor Keith laughed. Before the conversation ended, he invited Jackie and Jerry to attend a church picnic the following weekend. They came, and Jerry gently guided Jackie around as the church people introduced themselves. Jackie was totally blind. But in exactly two weeks, a guest evangelist was scheduled to speak at the church. When he came, he prayed for Jackie and her eyes immediately opened, two weeks nearly to the hour!

Since then, for the last three years Jackie has worked for the church, using the computer daily. That is just one of the many ways she and Jerry have been a blessing to the church. Her eyesight is perfect.

When Pastor Keith heard from the Lord that day, it was life-changing for Jackie. One thing is for sure—whatever the Holy Spirit says is true. He is the Spirit of Truth, and He will never lie. There is nothing more exciting on earth than to recognize that the Holy Spirit is talking to us daily. Pastor Keith's experience reminded me of the crippled man in the book of Acts:

> And in Lystra a certain man without strength in his feet was sitting, a cripple from his mother's womb, who had never walked. This man heard Paul speaking. Paul, observing him intently and seeing that he had faith to be healed, said with

a loud voice, "Stand up straight on your feet!" And he leaped and walked.

Acts 14:8–10

The Holy Spirit showed Paul that the man had faith to be made well. The knowledge was so strong that Paul boldly commanded the man to stand up, and he did. Paul got results when he spoke to the crippled man. We still see those kinds of powerful results today, for example when God spoke to Michelle through Pastor Michael and to Jackie through Pastor Keith. To God be the glory!

God's Words Are Creative

Everything God says is filled with creative power. Just as from the beginning, when God said, "Let there be light" (Genesis 1:3), the same Holy Spirit speaks things into existence in our lives. It is human nature to question and to second-guess our situation, but when the Holy Spirit talks to us, the results are guaranteed. His words are true and will come to pass.

Most every Christian who enjoys an intimate walk with God will begin the day with prayer and meditation, anticipating being drawn to a specific Scripture that contains a "message" the Holy Spirit is speaking to him or her that day. But it is possible to hear the Holy Spirit in many other ways as well. The bottom line is that we must have the "bread" of the Word of God, but we also must have communication and relationship with the Author.

When Jesus said to Simon, "Your name is rock" (*petras*; see Matthew 16:18), Peter was not acting like a rock. In fact, the name *Simon* means a reed blowing in the wind, unstable and vascillating. But as soon as Jesus changed Simon's name

22

to Peter (rock) it was a reality, although Peter did not act like a rock immediately. In fact, in most of His responses to Peter, Jesus rebuked him.

Ultimately, though, Peter acted like a rock. He was a rock when he laid his life on the line on the Day of Pentecost, announcing to the Israelites, "Jesus of Nazareth . . . being delivered by the determined purpose and foreknowledge of God, you have taken by lawless hands, have crucified, and put to death" (Acts 2:22–23). He was a rock when he confronted Ananias and Sapphira, saying, "Ananias, why has Satan filled your heart to lie to the Holy Spirit and keep back part of the price of the land for yourself?" (Acts 5:3). And he walked in God's authority when people were healed even by being under his shadow: "They brought the sick out into the streets and laid them on beds and couches, that at least the shadow of Peter passing by might fall on some of them" (Acts 5:15). In fact, more miracles are attributed to Peter's ministry than to any other disciple or apostle—all because Jesus prophesied to him, taking him from a reed to a rock.

What Is God Saying?

I would like to say to all preachers and Bible teachers, and really to all Christians, that we do not need more information, we need more understanding. We should not be as concerned about what God said yesterday as we should about having a fresh hunger for what He is saying today. Fresh understanding and insight from God is to the Church what new technology is to the business world. We need to hear the heart of God. Look at 1 Peter 4:11:

> If anyone speaks, let him speak as the oracles of God. If anyone ministers, let him do it as with the ability which God

supplies, that in all things God may be glorified through Jesus Christ, to whom belong the glory and the dominion forever and ever. Amen.

An oracle is something fresh that is coming from God. It is mandatory that we be listening to the Holy Spirit for the subject and emphasis He wants to bring out. Numerous pastors have told me excitedly, "The Lord has given me a wonderful 'word' for the people this weekend." Some pastors fall into a rut, however. Since they are not hearing the Holy Spirit, they drone on and on with an "old" message. Their message is not evil or false; it is merely lifeless because it is not coming from the heart of God for the present moment. It is out of season.

Following tradition is nothing more than honoring what God did at one time, but is no longer doing. In other words, religion honors what God did, but resists what He is doing. And many Christians practice "safe church" their entire lives, their attitude being, *God, don't make me pregnant with Your plan and purpose.*

Tradition is so deceptive. Many churches are in such a rut that you can set your watch with accuracy by when each step of a meeting or service happens. It becomes the same thing week after week, year after year. The freshness is gone. The Holy Spirit is limited to a back room, if He is allowed in at all. We need to make room for the Holy Spirit to move.

Spiritual Noise Pollution

One of the most diabolical strategies of our adversary, a strategy that keeps us from hearing the proceeding Word, is noise pollution. The enemy of our souls resists our experiencing this dimension of hearing God daily, so there is a war going on in the spirit world to keep us from hearing. The competition for listening and available ears is fierce. The devil is competing for our attention.

Just as McDonald's, Burger King and Subway compete for our business, the enemy "competes" with God for our attention. The battle is raging, and with so many technological advances available to us, we have to be more determined than ever to listen. Hundreds of television channels, the Internet, Facebook, Twitter, LinkedIn, iPods, MP3s, cell phones, computers, iPads and numerous other items of technological advancement compete for our attention. It seems as though everyone is preoccupied with some type of technology. But the world and all its stimuli have nothing to offer the inner man.

While God waits patiently for each of us to draw nigh to Him and pay the price of taking time to listen, the devil uses distractions, sensation, social media and all manner of ways to lure us, in order to keep our minds and hearts occupied with other things. We are inundated by noise pollution continually, yet to live triumphantly and productively within the Kingdom of God, people must listen to the King.

My passion is that Christians really know and discern the voice of the Holy Spirit. To learn to hear from God is the greatest asset any Christian can possess. Certainly everyone has seen misuses and abuses by those who claim to have heard God. However, no one stops spending money because there is counterfeit money out there. It should be part of normal Christianity to walk in fellowship with God intimately enough to enable us to hear from Him on a daily basis. Jesus did not say that His sheep would listen to CDs, read books or memorize Bible verses, although these things are all good. But He did say, "My sheep hear My voice, and I know them, and they follow Me" (John 10:27).

Well-intentioned Christians make "Kingdom" decisions that are derived from a human perspective and not God's. But I love a sign one pastor posted in his office: "For God so loved the world, that He didn't send a committee."

Hearing on the Inside

As I was seeking God about the need for quality of ministry in the Body of Christ, the Holy Spirit spoke these words: "When ministers are not led by the Spirit, they get into works."

Works become a substitute for living water. Jesus' words to Martha about that were compassionate but firm: "Martha, Martha, you are worried and troubled about many things. But *one thing* is needed, and Mary has chosen that good part, which will not be taken away from her" (Luke 10:41–42, emphasis added).

Martha had a need to feel useful and accepted. She had a need to be needed. She was not hearing the Holy Spirit inside her. Christians who are not hearing the proceeding word will always be caught up in performance, trying to satisfy that inward ache through religious accomplishment. There is nothing wrong with hard work and being a servant in the house of God, but it must be done with the right motive. Martha's motive was her need to be needed, and because she was not hearing and communing with the Holy Spirit, she lacked peace on the inside. She was struggling to find fulfillment through serving.

Something happens on the inside, though, when we begin to tune in and hear from God. Peace comes. Rest comes. No longer present are the nagging doubts about whether we are pleasing God, or the fears that God is disappointed in us. Gone is the feeling that we need to expend endless energy in order to gain God's approval.

Believers who are being honest with themselves are weary of expending energy on anything that God has not specifically called them to do. It is time we realize that each of us has different callings and that we are not obligated to be a jack-of-all-trades working to meet any possible need in the Kingdom of God. Feeling obligated to try to function in areas we are not called to leaves us feeling guilty and unsatisfied. I have to remind myself that not everything has my name on it. I can only aim for what God has called me to do. What an awesome freedom—to do only what He is calling each of us to do. We are only anointed to do our specific part.

> Grow up in all things into Him who is the head—Christ—from whom the whole body, joined and knit together by what every joint supplies, according to the effective working by which *every part does its share*, causes growth of the body for the edifying of itself in love.
>
> Ephesians 4:15–16, emphasis added

Paul proclaimed in 2 Timothy 4:7 that he had finished his course. I do not desire to follow Paul's course. I want to follow and fulfill the course to which God has called me. That is the course in which I will experience the grace and fulfillment of God. It will bring fulfillment that is too wonderful to put into words.

How do I know the course God has put before me so that I can follow it and accomplish what He has called me to do? By hearing His voice. We have looked at two ways we can do that so far—by hearing Him speak through the written Word, the Bible, and by hearing Him speak through the proceeding Word. Let's go on from here to look at several other specific ways in which God speaks to us.

2

Hearing God through His Thoughts

*Fasting from our own thoughts and opinions creates a
pathway to hearing God clearly.*

One day recently, a person came to mind whom I had not
thought of for over thirty years. Several times that day, I remi-
nisced over conversations we had had years ago. Then out of
the blue, the following day that person contacted me. I was
amazed. Obviously, the Holy Spirit was giving me His thoughts
about this man, knowing that he was going to contact me.

I believe all Christians have these types of experiences,
but they usually go unnoticed and unacknowledged. God is
speaking all the time, however, and we will hear Him more
if we stop to acknowledge these "coincidences" and praise
Him for communicating with us.

I have learned two significant truths from such experiences.
First of all, the Lord is letting us know He is active in our lives

(and in our thoughts). Second, we can expect to hear His voice more frequently if we exercise a willingness to pay attention.

What is hearing from God? Hearing Him is no less than knowing what is on His mind. This should be a way of life for the Christian and part of our experience. God willingly gives His thoughts and His mind to those who desire to listen to Him. Scripture says He declares His thoughts to us: "For behold, he who forms mountains, and creates the wind, *who declares to man what his thought is*, and makes the morning darkness, who treads the high places of the earth—the LORD God of hosts is His name" (Amos 4:13, emphasis added).

It appears that although God wants to give us His thoughts, many people ignore, reject and refuse them. As Micah 4:11–12 says, "Many nations . . . do not know the thoughts of the LORD, nor do they understand His counsel."

How amazing it is that God directs a huge number of His thoughts toward us. "How precious also are Your thoughts to me, O God! How great is the sum of them!" (Psalm 139:17).

God promises to include us in what He is doing. As the prophet Amos said, "Surely the Lord GOD does nothing, unless He reveals His secret to His servants the prophets" (Amos 3:7).

In Tune with God

Hearing God's thoughts is an assurance that we are in tune with Him. During the first few months after I received the Holy Spirit, I was amazed at how the Holy Spirit spoke to people. For example, my sister was standing at her kitchen sink one morning in 1968 and clearly heard the Lord's voice tell her, "Robert Kennedy is going to be assassinated."

That horrendous incident happened three weeks later. I know the Lord loved that man, but we live in a fallen world where deplorable things happen. Yet nothing catches God off guard or by surprise. He sees and knows all things, and He makes His people aware of events—I believe for the purpose of prayer.

One lady who was my mentor for many years heard the Lord speak this to her one day: "Martin Luther King is going to be assassinated." Three years before it happened, she stood up in church and related what she had heard, and then asked her church to pray. The more we pay attention to these kinds of thoughts, the more we realize that this is a common way God communicates things to us. God includes us and lets us in on things because we are in relationship with Him.

A friend of mine pastors a church in Indiana. One man in his church often has these experiences of hearing the thoughts of God—usually while he is mowing his lawn. A few years ago he received one of God's thoughts: "Not one hurricane will hit the United States this year." And in that year no hurricanes hit, although ironically, the media had been saying it would be the worst hurricane season ever. This man prays a lot about the weather, and God talks to him about it. Many times the Lord will show this man whether it will be a very cool or very dry year, or if it will rain up until June, but not rain after that. I believe the Lord speaks to him just because he has an interest in the weather and prays about it.

God's Thoughts

Hearing the thoughts of God is probably one of the foremost ways the Holy Spirit speaks to you and me. In fact, God will interject His thoughts into our daily lives. This is meant to be a daily occurrence for the believer, but often we do not recognize it as God talking to us, because we are expecting something sensational and earthshaking.

Have you ever had someone on your mind, and then found out later that the person was going through some difficulty and really needed prayer? Or in marriage a husband will be thinking of something, and seconds later his wife will begin talking about the same subject. Christian couples marvel at how often this happens. We need to recognize that this is just one way the Holy Spirit is communicating, by interjecting His thoughts into our spirit. Many times we hear the Lord without even realizing it, probably because it comes so naturally. Because of this, we do not always give God credit for good experiences, failing to realize that He inspired our course of action. His direction often comes to us when He interjects His thoughts into our spirit.

Walking into a certain church for the first time years ago, I did not even know who the pastor was. Finally, when he stood up to speak, the Holy Spirit said, "Gestapo." I knew immediately that the Lord was saying this pastor had huge control issues. In the following years, this proved amazingly accurate. He had the most dominating personality I have ever witnessed in a leader. Did the Lord love this pastor? Absolutely. But the man's extreme insecurities resulted in an extreme need to control. Eventually people began to see it, and his congregation of hundreds dwindled down to a few. The church building was sold, and another pastor took the remaining few to start with a new beginning.

The sad thing is that to this day, this pastor does not recognize his own "demons" and is unwilling to face the fact that he has a problem. He still goes about acting as if what happened was the people's fault. But my hearing the word was simply God sharing His thoughts with me—not so that I would be critical, but rather so that I would pray. God had declared to me what He thought about the situation, as Amos 4:13 says.

An Agitated Mind Cannot Hear

Have you ever dealt with a child who is upset? For example, if he breaks a toy, he may cry in anger and frustration. Since you are the parent, you have good news for the child—you plan to fix the toy. However, in his agitated state the child cannot hear the good news until you get him to stop crying. You have to stop the anguish first.

Maybe at times we simply cannot hear the Lord because we are in a state of stress and worry, full of the cares of the world. An agitated mind is a barrier to the thoughts of God. Think about when Moses gave good news to the people of Israel who had been in bondage, but they could not hear (receive) from Moses because of their anguish:

> Therefore say to the children of Israel: "I am the LORD; I will bring you out from under the burdens of the Egyptians, I will rescue you from their bondage, and I will redeem you with an outstretched arm and with great judgments. . . ."
> So Moses spoke thus to the children of Israel; but they did not heed Moses, because of anguish of spirit and cruel bondage.
>
> Exodus 6:6, 9

Our agitated mind becomes a barricade to God's thoughts; it is not the devil who is the barrier. The devil has been defeated through the cross and only has the ability to lie and deceive. Our real problem is our analytical (and overanxious) mind. When struggling with anxiety or worry, it is good to stop and take time to worship God. Worship invites His presence and His peace. God speaks in peace, not strife. Raging emotions block the Holy Spirit.

Is It God's Thought?

To say that God communicates to us through His thoughts is not to say that any thought that enters our mind is automatically a thought from God. Sometimes they are simply our thoughts—maybe a good idea, but not a God idea. Obviously, we must be careful to examine ourselves and judge all thoughts through the Holy Spirit to determine whether they are indeed merely inspiration (from ourselves), understanding (from God) or are solely from the devil. John said, "Beloved, do not believe every spirit, but test the spirits, whether they are of God; because many false prophets have gone out into the world" (1 John 4:1).

How can you know if your thought came from God? Here is what I have learned: *A thought from God is not part of your thinking process.* When God drops or interjects a thought into your spirit, it has nothing to do with *your* thinking or rationalizing. He puts the thought into your spirit, bypassing your brain. For example, you may see a car pass by that reminds you of a car your friend drives, which makes you think of that person. That is a thought process, and it was the car that made you think of your friend. However, when the Lord speaks to you, His thought is just suddenly there—unrelated to anything you were doing or thinking. You then recognize such a thought is from the Lord, because it was "dropped in."

The devil, on the other hand, can also work through your thought process. He wars against the mind and sends fiery darts of wicked and worrisome thoughts (see Ephesians 6). The nature of the devil is to torment you and to bring unrest. Demonic thoughts provoke worry and anxiety and rob you of peace. His thoughts come as speculation and imagination: *What if this happens? What if I've made the wrong decision . . . ?*

There is no one who has not experienced such thoughts.

In fact, many people are tormented in their thought lives. Yet God designed our thought lives as an awesome way that He communicates to us. It stands to reason that the devil attempts to copy what God does; he tries to hijack the very method God uses. The enemy is a great counterfeiter and gives us his thoughts so deceptively that we do not realize we are being barraged by the enemy. In other words, he throws his thoughts at us and then accuses us of having those thoughts ourselves—thoughts that were never ours in the first place.

As we grow in wisdom and choose to live more aggressively as Christians, we can live victoriously by always standing guard against these speculations of the enemy, as Paul so plainly stated in 2 Corinthians 10:4–5:

> For the weapons of our warfare are not carnal but mighty in God for pulling down strongholds, casting down arguments and every high thing that exalts itself against the knowledge of God, bringing every thought into captivity to the obedience of Christ.

Fast from Your Thoughts

If you are a person who has to be right on every subject, you might have trouble accepting God's voice. There is nothing wrong with wanting to be right, but the problem is *having to be right*. The bottom line is that God is smarter than we are. Many times we do not hear God because our mind is too full of our own thoughts. We may be guilty of being far too opinionated, especially on certain topics.

One way to hear more from the Holy Spirit is to fast from our own thoughts. Yes, there is a better fast to go on than a fast from food. We can fast from our own thoughts and opinions. Isaiah proclaimed that we can fast from other things besides food when he declared these words of the Lord: "Take away the yoke from your midst, the pointing of the finger, and speaking wickedness" (Isaiah 58:9).

Jesus is our example. He lived a perpetual fast from His own thoughts and opinions. He emphasized this truth continually. In John 5:19 He said, "Most assuredly, I say to you, the Son can do nothing of Himself, but what He sees the Father do; for whatever He does, the Son also does in like manner." And in John 14:10 He said, "The words that I speak to you I do not speak on My own authority [initiative]; but the Father who dwells in Me does the works."

As Christians we *can* go on a determined fast for the rest of our lives. We can choose to live a perpetual fast from our own thoughts and opinions. This creates a wonderful freedom and leaves us open to hear God's input on any subject. We also need to repent of stubbornness, which is nothing more than making idols of our own opinions. All idolatry is sin. "Therefore, my beloved, flee from idolatry" (1 Corinthians 10:14). "For rebellion is as the sin of witchcraft, and stubbornness is as iniquity and idolatry" (1 Samuel 15:23).

Nothing will hinder hearing God more than when we are opinionated or critical. We have to live neutrally, without a critical and judgmental spirit. Our opinion does not count, even if we are popular. To hear what God is saying, we must look at every situation without bias or speculation.

What does God want from us? Look at the words of Jesus in Matthew 8:19–20, when a certain scribe approached Jesus. The man was making a decision to follow Him, but he did not get the answer from Jesus he was expecting: "Then a certain scribe came and said to Him, 'Teacher, I will follow You wherever You go.' And Jesus said to him, 'Foxes have holes and birds of the air have nests, but the Son of Man has nowhere to lay His head.'"

You would think Jesus would have commended the man and congratulated him. But instead He said that "the Son of Man has nowhere to lay His head." For years I did not understand this, but I believe that clearly what Jesus was saying is that if we want to follow Him, He is looking for a place to lay His head—that is, He wants to remove our head (our opinion and will) and replace it with His head. Jesus was pointing out to that scribe the price he must pay. The man would not have the luxury of following his own opinion and agenda or remaining the head of his own life; he would have to allow Jesus to become the head and depend on Him.

God Interrupts Our Thoughts

Many times we Christians are so quick to give our opinions that we leave no room for God's mind in certain matters. Wouldn't it be refreshing if someone asked us what we thought about the latest trend, and we just replied, "I don't know"?

That response might surprise the person, and he or she might ask, "Why don't you know?"

"I don't know because I haven't heard the Lord say anything to me about it," we could answer.

Jesus said it plainly: "I can of Myself do nothing. As I hear, I judge; and My judgment is righteous, because I do not seek My *own* will but the will of the Father who sent Me" (John 5:30, emphasis added).

A perfect example of this is when the scribes and Pharisees approached Jesus concerning a woman they had caught in adultery. They asked Him for His judgment on what they should do with her. Rather than quickly answering them, it seems He was fasting from His own thoughts as He stooped down and wrote on the ground.

When Jesus stood up, He spoke the thoughts of God: "He who is without sin among you, let him throw a stone at her first" (John 8:7). Jesus made Himself available to hear what the Father was saying.

Someone might say, "Doesn't God give us common sense and critical thinking skills and expect us to use them?"

Absolutely. But when the Lord wants to speak to our spirit, He overrides our reasoning process. He is not expecting us to live with our mind in neutral, but He wants us to be willing to receive His thoughts. While we recognize that our mind is a gift from God, we also have to receive what He is saying in our inner man.

We do not want to use our reasoning mind against God. Romans 8:7 says that "the carnal [natural] mind is enmity against God; for it is not subject to the law of God, nor indeed can be." This statement was written to Christians. We have to surrender our analytical mind to Him. He wants us to have the mind of Christ. "For 'who has known the mind of the LORD that he may instruct Him?' But we have the mind of Christ" (1 Corinthians 2:16).

Higher, but Not Unattainable

When we initially read Isaiah's account of God's thoughts in Isaiah 55:8–9, we automatically place God's thoughts on an impossible and unreachable plateau: "'For My thoughts are not your thoughts, nor are your ways My ways,' says the LORD. 'For as the heavens are higher than the earth, so are My ways higher than your ways, and My thoughts than your thoughts.'"

Contrary to what we are inclined to believe, His thoughts are not unattainable, and they are not off-limits. He wants to share His thoughts with us so that we see life from His perspective. We cannot think God's thoughts, however, and be consumed with our own thoughts as well. The key is to live in His presence and dwell on Him continually.

One day during my years as a pastor, I was in my car on the way to church. As I reached up to turn the radio on, I heard the Holy Spirit say, "Turn it off."

I immediately explained to Him that it was tuned to Christian radio. He was unimpressed.

He spoke again to my inner man, "I'm tired of you letting someone else do your worshiping for you."

In other words, He wanted me to use that driving time to sing to Him and worship Him directly. I repented.

This habit of meditating and worshiping while driving has since become a blessing. Many times the Lord will drop His thoughts into my spirit simply because I am *making room* for His thoughts. God never makes it complicated. He makes things simple. We only have to make room for Him to speak.

In fact, hearing a song in my spirit has been a common experience for me. Many mornings I will wake up hearing a song. Sometimes it is a familiar spiritual song, but other times it is a secular song with certain words that God is speaking directly to me. The song will rise up in my spirit, giving me a message straight from God's heart. One morning in particular, I heard a portion of the secular song titled "I'm into Something Good." And I was! Something very good happened that day.

One time when I was in a struggle, I woke up one morning hearing a line from the old song "Nothing Is Impossible." Its message is that when we put our trust in God, nothing is impossible. I knew immediately that God was telling me to trust Him for the impossible.

Another time I had been going through a difficult time, and in my spirit I could hear the song, "Oh, What a Beautiful

Mornin'" by Rodgers and Hammerstein. Hours later things begin to change, and the next two days were wonderful.

You Are Not Separated from God

Christians often live in an illusion of separation from God. We receive little from the Holy Spirit if, instead of acknowledging His presence within our spirit, we perceive God as living in a distant land somewhere. When Elijah spoke to King Ahab, he addressed him this way: "As the LORD God of Israel lives, *before whom I stand*, there shall not be dew nor rain these years, except at my word" (1 Kings 17:1, emphasis added). In effect, he was saying that although he was standing before Ahab, he was also (right then) standing in the presence of Almighty God.

How much more, under the New Covenant, are we not only standing before God, but are we *in* Christ and He is *in* us? Countless Scriptures describe this covenant relationship. When this becomes a revelation to us, no longer do we see God at a distance, but instead we know that He dwells within. *Nothing* is impossible with Him, and we can easily think *His thoughts*.

Colossians 2:10 tells us, "And you are complete in Him, who is the head of all principality and power." The devil (and wrong teaching) have sabotaged the Christian from the reality that God, through Jesus Christ and the power of the Holy Spirit, is working within us 24/7. Begin now to ask the Lord to give you His thoughts. Repent from being opinionated or preoccupied or distracted, and start expecting right now to hear Him more.

Now we have looked at three ways we can hear from God—through the Word (the Bible), through the proceeding word, and through hearing His thoughts. In the next chapter, we will look another way God speaks to us—through the word of knowledge.

3

Hearing God through Words of Knowledge

You can know that you know. . . .

> But the manifestation of the Spirit is given to each one for the profit of all: for to one is given the word of wisdom through the Spirit, *to another the word of knowledge through the same Spirit.*
>
> 1 Corinthians 12:7–8, emphasis added

One Sunday morning in a Houston church, I was blessed as the Holy Spirit gave me a word of knowledge. I cannot explain it, but suddenly I was just full of knowledge that there was a woman present for whom two previous pregnancies had been very difficult, and she was pregnant again. But the knowledge was also that this pregnancy would not be difficult. I was so excited that I asked whoever it was to raise her hand. No one responded. Again I repeated what the Lord was showing me, but got no response. Feeling a little embarrassed, I was thankful for my round-trip ticket. I flew home to Alabama the following day.

On Tuesday, the pastor called me excitedly and asked, "Remember the word about the woman who was pregnant?"

"I sure do," I replied.

He continued, "She was there in the meeting Sunday, but she didn't know she was pregnant! Yesterday she took a test and found out it was indeed true."

The exciting thing about this story was that in the following months, she had a trouble-free pregnancy (unlike her previous experiences). In fact, the day her water broke, her husband went to put things in the car to take her to the hospital, but before he could get her into the car, she had the baby in the master bedroom. God fulfills His word!

My experience in receiving that word had nothing to do with intelligence or figuring something out. It was simply the Holy Spirit giving me a specific word of knowledge that He wanted to minister to this woman. One of the nine gifts of the Holy Spirit is the word of knowledge. When God gives us a word of knowledge, the only way to explain it is that one minute you do not know it, and the next minute you know it. It is one of the wonderful ways we can hear the voice of the Holy Spirit. When it happens, you just "know that you know" something is true. It is an intuitiveness that cannot be explained . . . you just *know*.

God's Downloads

I have heard people try to explain the word of knowledge as something we learn or are trained to receive. That is absolutely false. Getting a word of knowledge is not something we learn. A word of knowledge is when God drops in or "downloads" into our spirit knowledge that we did not previously have.

Recently an attorney reminded me of an instance that occurred when I was speaking at his church in Alabama. He reminded me that as I had looked at him, I had suddenly had knowledge from the Lord, and I had said, "Brother, I don't know what health problem you are having, but it is not unto death."

In that small window of knowledge, I just knew something was wrong with him, but that he would be okay. When he talked to me recently, he filled me in on his testimony, which exactly matched the word of knowledge.

"After having my heart rhythm restored twice by electrical shock, I developed the same symptoms again within a very short period of time," he told me. "The cardiologist I was seeing said it was not my heart and refused to see me again for four months. My strength deteriorated to the point that I would have to stop and rest before I could walk inside the gas station from a pump to pay. I continued to get weaker. I tried to make appointments with other cardiologists, but the wait was months before they could see me. At that point, it did not look as if I would be alive for even one more month. You came to our Alabama church, and in the middle of your message you stopped, looked at me and said, 'Brother, I don't know what health problem you are having, but it is not unto death.' That word was so encouraging because my wife and I were both feeling so helpless.

"Weeks later, my wife found a number on the Internet for the head cardiac electrophysiologist at Cleveland Clinic. The doctor saw me and immediately said he thought my problem was as simple as low blood. I had taken blood thinner and apparently had lost a lot of blood. I had a blood test and found out my blood level was severely low. After two blood infusions, I have been fine. The word you delivered was not only timely and encouraging; it literally gave us new hope and faith to keep on searching and fighting."

Knowing the Mind of the Lord

Receiving knowledge from the Lord is probably the most common way that we hear from Him. Just as a husband and wife often seem to know one another's thoughts, we can know God and know His thoughts because of our relationship with Him. "Now we have received, not the spirit of the world, but the Spirit who is from God, that we might know the things that have been freely given to us by God" (1 Corinthians 2:12).

God wants to communicate to us in this way. We can know what is on His mind. "However, when He, the Spirit of truth, has come, He will guide you into all truth; for He will not speak on His own authority, but whatever He hears He will speak; and He will tell you things to come" (John 16:13).

Most often, the knowledge God gives comes to us intuitively. Women can probably identify with this truth more easily than men, because they are usually more intuitive by nature. Knowledge rarely comes with fireworks. It is more of a "knowing." Most of us can remember times when God gave us knowledge and we dismissed it because of the slightness of it, only to find out later that it was God speaking to us.

Obviously, when God communicates to any of us, He does not need to process anything through our brains, but gives knowledge by His Spirit to our spirit. He created our intellect to function as a servant, not a master or governor. God created us in such a way that we hear and commune with Him by way of the Holy Spirit. Our human spirits are like receivers that begin to know and understand more and more intuitively what is the mind of the Holy Spirit. As we mature in the Lord, we learn to trust the impulses, checkings and witnesses of the Holy Spirit.

In my third year of full-time ministry, I was invited by a small group of people to begin a church in Beaumont, Texas. We began meeting on Sundays in a rented room of the Ramada Inn, and we gathered in a home for our midweek meeting. We had lived in the city only a short time when we discovered that a Jewish synagogue in a prime location was up for sale. We were able to purchase it for an extremely reasonable price and received financing from a local bank.

After we had taken possession of the building and had enjoyed seeing the Lord add new faces, we felt that He was stretching our vision. One of the first things the Holy Spirit spoke was that we were to have a prophet's room built onto the church to house guest evangelists. The church began to pray and seek direction about the addition. We knew we needed a miracle, as we had no capital available. The command from the Lord continued to stir our spirits. Some suggested that we simply park a trailer by the church (to save God the money), but the Lord continued to prompt us to trust Him for the addition.

A few weeks after everyone began to pray, I was in the car on an errand. As I was driving, I suddenly blurted out loud, "Thank You, Lord, for five thousand dollars." Then I thought to myself, *What a ridiculous statement!*

A few days later as I was driving to church, the same thing happened. I heard myself declaring the same statement again:

"Thank You, Lord, for five thousand dollars." I had no idea why I said it and just brushed the statement off.

Later that week, a man in the church came to me and handed me a check, saying, "This is for your prophets' room. My wife and I felt the Lord told us to give it to you."

I thanked him and walked away, and then I saw that the check was for exactly five thousand dollars.

Always Creative

My experience in the car, hearing those words coming out of my mouth, was an example of God giving me knowledge. When God gives a word of knowledge, it is *always creative*. The knowledge is from the mind of God; it is something He intends to do. His word always has creative power accompanying it. Whatever the word is, it already exists in His mind. This is exciting because whenever we hear the Lord speak to us in this way, His creative power is released. Our only role is to agree with Him.

Many times this happens in dialogue or basic conversation. God reserves the right to interrupt conversation among Christians and insert a creative word of knowledge. As Christians, when we begin to acknowledge and believe that we are living in the presence of the Lord, we will experience more evidence of His abiding presence. He abides in us; He does not come and go: "But the anointing which you have received from Him abides in you" (1 John 2:27).

If we fail to realize that we are living in God's presence, we miss out on the awesome adventure He has in store for us. What we must do as Christians is *acknowledge His abiding presence*. It is not complicated. We must accept that He is with us at all times and is as close as our own breath.

The amazing thing about God is that He is just there. His presence is authentic and tangible, but not necessarily sensational. The more we walk with a consciousness of His presence, the more we will realize that He is speaking. We can be in tune with knowledge He is expressing to us. His words are creative.

Receiving Knowledge

While I was praying for some friends of mine who travel as evangelists, the Lord spoke the word *restitution*. I contacted them and told them the word that the Holy Spirit had spoken. However, they were perplexed about what it was the Lord was referring to.

Then a few months later, they encountered a serious mechanical problem with their travel trailer, which also serves as their home. The problem was such that it incapacitated the trailer, making it impossible for them to fulfill their speaking engagements. As they approached the dealer, he refused to help. By doing some checking around, however, they discovered that the trailer had been sold to them at an illegal weight for the type of axles on it. They approached the state government about the legal weight limit, which put pressure on the dealer. The dealer was forced to make restitution and refunded their money. As a result, they were able to replace their travel home with a much safer one.

During this ordeal, the Lord brought back to them the word He had spoken. Although for a period of time things did not look good, they were able to stand on the word *restitution* that God had given. Before they knew there would be a problem, God was already watching out for them. He gave them a word, and it came to pass.

Trust the Holy Spirit

The more we grow spiritually, the more we know that we can always trust the Holy Spirit inside us. He gives us an unshakeable, deep-down knowing that will ring true, even if a prophet or a friend stands before us and tells us otherwise.

The Holy Spirit can be trusted. He has promised that He will never lie to the believer. We can choose to be stubborn and put more confidence in our emotions or in the convincing persuasion of another person, but God is committed to telling us the truth. He is the Spirit of Truth.

The Holy Spirit in your inner being will never lead you astray. When you receive the Holy Spirit, you receive the Spirit of Truth. Trust what you are hearing from Him on the inside.

So far, we have seen that God speaks to us through the Bible and the proceeding word, through His thoughts in our minds and through words of knowledge. Now let's look at another way He speaks to us, by speaking words into our spirit.

4

Hearing God through His Words in Your Spirit

One word from God settles all manner of issues.

> Your ears shall hear a word behind you, say-
> ing, "This is the way, walk in it," whenever
> you turn to the right hand or whenever you
> turn to the left.

Isaiah 30:21

It was early on a Saturday morning when I took my teenage daughter, Brittani, to the airport in Birmingham, Alabama. With happy visions of vacationing and snowboarding, she was flying to Montana to visit my sister and her family. We successfully checked her bags on Southwest Airlines, and I was pleased with how smoothly everything was going.

Suddenly, it hit me that Brittani would have to change airlines in Portland to fly to Missoula, Montana. Only then did I realize that her bags were checked only as far as Portland. She would have to retrieve her bags, then recheck them onto this small airline for the ride to Montana. I checked her itinerary, and she had a very short layover between planes. That meant that she would not only be in this huge, unfamiliar airport, but that she would have little time to make this all happen. Fear gripped me as I thought, *It will take a miracle for her to make it!* I felt as if I had sent Brittani into an impossible situation. As I began the drive home from the airport, I prayed earnestly for the Lord to help her. Instantly, a song rose up in me, the familiar old hymn "Great Is Thy Faithfulness." I knew the Holy Spirit was speaking (singing) to me about His faithfulness. Peace flooded my whole being. I knew hearing that song meant the Lord would be faithful to help my daughter.

Hours later, Brittani called me after safely arriving in Montana. She told me that when she arrived in Portland, she went to the carousel to get her bag and it was the first one off. She took it to the other airline, checked in and boarded the plane with a few minutes to spare.

I stood again amazed at God. I have flown on airlines for decades, and my bag has never been the first one off. Not once. In fact, mine are always nearly the last.

Exactly the Words We Need

The Lord always speaks exactly the words we need to hear. In chapter 2, I talked about how we can hear God as He gives us His thoughts in our mind, but in this chapter I want to explain how we can hear God as He gives us words and phrases in our spirit. These two ways of hearing Him are different in that one is simply having a thought that we recognize comes from Him, while the other is actually hearing a word or phrase in our spirit, the way I heard that hymn when I was praying for my daughter about her travels.

In this chapter, let me tell you some more examples of hearing His words in your spirit. For example, one night in a small church in an Indiana town, I felt the Lord wanted me to pray for a couple who were sitting toward the back of the church. As I prayed for them, I heard the Holy Spirit say three words in my spirit: "Pennies from heaven."

I assumed that the words were God's metaphor saying He was going to bless their finances. Exactly ten months later, this couple came to a meeting I was at in the same church. I stood in awe as they told me their experience. Following that night, they immediately had begun to find pennies and other coins. They found them in their car, on the street, between the cushions of the couch, everywhere. They told me how they would put them in rolls and take them to the bank, and then later the same day they would find even more. Ultimately, in those ten months they collected enough coins to pay for a coveted trip to Israel. Those three words, "pennies from heaven," were life-changing for them, and who would have thought that the Lord would fulfill the word He had given in the most literal sense?

Speaking at an organization in Arkansas that helps abused women, I was amazed at how receptive the women were to the Holy Spirit's presence. It was so sweet the way God gave a specific word that afternoon for one of the women. She had requested prayer, and while we were praying, words of encouragement flowed out of me concerning her. The word *target* came up in my spirit several times for her, regarding her life being on target and the Lord helping her hit the target. A number of the women began to laugh at this, and finally one of them spoke out, "She works at Target!"

At a Missouri youth camp, a teenage girl named Carla came to the altar for prayer. During the prayer, the Lord gently said to her that He had had His hand on her since she was in her mother's womb. The word really encouraged her. But even more amazing was that her mother happened to be present in the meeting. She came to me and told me that sixteen years earlier, when she was pregnant with Carla, she was on her way to the abortion clinic because she did not feel she could handle raising a child. On the way, the Lord had spoken clearly to her, telling her not to abort her baby.

Hearing an Audible Voice

Does God speak to us in an audible voice? I have never heard God's voice audibly. I am not saying that He does not speak audibly; I have heard some claim that they have experienced that. But I believe it is a rare occurrence because hearing an audible voice from God would not be hearing words in your spirit, but rather with your physical ears. When the Holy Spirit communicates with you and me, He talks to our inner man and not to our brain.

I will say that there are times when a word from God is so clear that it almost seems audible. For example, when I was a young pastor still in my twenties, I awoke out of sleep one morning and heard these inaudible but clear words from the Holy Spirit: "Those looking to heaven are missing it." There was a pause, and then He spoke again: "I'm looking for those who have the living water flowing through them."

I have never forgotten those words. This is clearly one of the ways the Holy Spirit speaks—in a word or a brief sentence. Nearly all of these instances are rather slight, but are always distinct. There is a manner in which the Holy Spirit speaks that makes you know that the phrase you heard was not merely your own thought.

Although God's voice comes to you almost imperceptible in volume, there is an authenticity to it that rings true in your spirit. When you hear Him speak, it is not so much hearing a voice as it is hearing words.

My first experiences of hearing God's words in my spirit happened during the summers while I was in college. I attended a church known for its depth of worship—the Evangelistic Center in Kansas City, Missouri. During the worship portion of the service, I would hear words in my spirit relating to physical afflictions such as stomach issues, kidney problems and so forth. Although I was not sure what to do with this knowledge, I would listen intently. A few minutes later, one of the pastors would declare that God desired to heal people of various afflictions—the same illnesses I was hearing in my spirit. I learned that this was God's way of letting me know I was indeed hearing His voice.

I had similar experiences concerning the gift of prophecy. I would hear a phrase that I felt I was to prophesy, but I was too timid to give it forth. Then seconds later, another person would give the same or a very similar message. Either that or what I had heard would be the subject on which the sermon was centered. I wanted to kick myself for not speaking out, but then I began to realize that God is an encourager. He always assures us that we are hearing His voice, and we can determine on the next opportunity to step out in faith and obey. Later on, I gained confidence and was able to move beyond my timidity to trust what I was hearing Him say and speak it out.

One Sunday morning in a Florida church where I was speaking, there were about five hundred people present. As I was making final remarks, I felt prompted by the Lord to pray over a man sitting with his wife near the aisle. I prayed a brief prayer of blessing over them. Then looking at the man, I commented, "The only thing I heard when praying for you were the words *full speed ahead.*"

A few minutes later, the pastor stood up to close the meeting in prayer, and smiling, he said, "Steve doesn't know that the man he just spoke to is a professional race car driver!"

Even more amazing about this story is that this man had been asking direction from the Lord about whether he was to continue his racing career. He had lost a sponsorship and was considering an offer from another sponsor.

Months later, at a meeting in Kentucky I felt moved on by the Lord to pray for the pastor's ten-year-old son. As I prayed a quick prayer, I felt strongly that the Lord was giving that boy His authority. I spoke it out, and then for some reason I playfully added, "Like the cowboy, John Wayne."

After the meeting that evening, I went with several people to a gathering at the pastor's home. He invited me to see his son's bedroom, and as I entered I was amazed to see a life-sized cardboard cutout of John Wayne. I know that boy will never forget how the Holy Spirit spoke to him, letting him know how intimately He knew him. I had added that comment thinking I was being funny, but God was touching the boy's heart through those words.

At a church heavily involved in a building program, they were hoping for the miracle of being in the new building by Christmas. This was the month of June. Praying about their goal, I heard the Holy Spirit say the word *lickety-split*. To everyone's amazement, they ended up being in their new building in October. God is awesome.

Hearing Sentences from God

I love to worship and I enjoy a variety of worship music, so when I was only a few years in the ministry, I decided to ask the Lord one day if He would give me a worship song that would be sung all over the world. I do not know why I prayed that way, but it seemed like a good idea at the time. A couple hours later, I thought I would relax a little bit, so I stretched out on the couch in our Texas home.

I must have dozed off for a few minutes, but as I woke up, I heard the Lord's voice saying, "I'm not your music teacher."

Immediately I knew what He was saying to me. He had not called me to write music. Simply put, He was saying, "Don't waste your energy on something I have not called you to do."

Although the Lord's quick answer surprised me, I actually felt relieved. That experience has stayed with me my entire ministry. If God has not called me to do something, why would I want to do it?

That word from God helped me understand more completely Jesus' words in Matthew 11:29–30, "Take My yoke upon you and learn from Me, for I am gentle and lowly in heart, and you will find rest for your souls. For My yoke is easy and My burden is light." In other words, something is easy if He has called you to it. As individuals, we are only called to do that which He has yoked us to. Plainly, He has not called me to write music. But He has called me to preach and write. Whatever He calls us to is a pleasure, not a burden.

But if you are not called to do something and you try to do it anyway, it becomes a burden.

At one point as our family was growing, we were praying fervently that the Lord would help us find a house. Around that time I was preaching in Brooklyn, New York. While I was waiting on the Lord, preparing for the meeting, I asked the Lord again about a house.

As I prayed in that Brooklyn motel room, I heard the Holy Spirit say, "It will be a few more minutes."

It did not take much interpretation to understand that this meant it would be very soon. Exactly three weeks later, we put a contract on a home that God had led us to in a marvelous way. This was obviously a creative word from God, because we had already tried everything we could think of to find a suitable place.

The Lord's words often bring us wisdom and insight wherever we need it. During my years as a pastor, I went through a struggle of desiring recognition by other ministers. I could not understand why I was not invited to more conferences to speak, especially since I had written several books. It seemed that the Lord was going out of His way to hide me. I continued to seek the Lord about this, fervently praying and calling out to Him.

One morning during this time, I heard Him speak one sentence to me: "I have My eye on you."

Immediately, I was overcome with His love and an assurance of His hand upon me. For weeks following that experience, every time I would try to tell someone about the sentence the Holy Spirit spoke to me, I would begin to cry. At the time I did not know why I was moved to tears, but looking back, it is obvious that I needed to be more broken before Him. My spirit knew what my mind did not know.

Another time, arriving at a Wisconsin city where the annual conference for a large, nondenominational Christian organization was being held, I immediately went to my motel room and began to intercede for our meeting that night. At one point I stopped praying and was waiting in God's presence.

A few minutes passed, and then I heard the Holy Spirit gently ask me a question: "Do you know why they don't have the gold?"

I knew He was speaking to me about the people I would address in a few hours. I also knew that the gold He was referring to pertained to their spiritual richness in God (and their lack of it).

I answered Him, "No."

A few moments passed and He spoke again, answering His own question: "They welcome Me, but they don't follow Me."

During the following two days at the conference, I became well aware of what the Lord was saying. The people were enthusiastic, but without obedience.

In another instance, one evening I was conversing with a man following a meeting, and I heard these words for him concerning his job: "God has your back."

The man managed a very successful restaurant, and I did not know until later that he went to the pastor and said, "Why would Steve say that to me? I have a great job, and I'm very happy there."

A short time later, this man made a playful statement to an employee at work. He meant absolutely nothing by it; it was intended as a joke. To his surprise, however, the employee went to the HR department and reported it, and this manager was fired immediately. He was devastated, but he remembered the word I had given, "God has your back."

Within a few weeks, the Lord opened a door for another job with double the pay. The new job is one he loves and enjoys.

Listening Ears

More and more, it is obvious to me that hearing from God should be normal and commonplace for the Christian. Truthfully, our minds are so loud and preoccupied that we do not leave room for God to speak. Prayer is mostly listening. The hardest part of prayer is praying until you feel your spirit break through into God's presence. Then comes rest. Anxious thoughts begin to fade, and you become available to hear what is being spoken in the Godhead.

As Christians, we should realize that hearing from God is a normal daily occurrence, just as communicating with our mate or closest friend would be. Prayer should be a two-way conversation, and listening to God must become a *habit*. We must learn to be less analytical and to live with more attentiveness to the Holy Spirit. Our carnal minds love to analyze, gossip and worry. But the mind of the Spirit is peace, and He is available at all times. The great news is that we do not have to get religious to hear Him; we just need to be open.

I once asked the Lord, "Why don't You speak louder?" (It seems like a question many people want to ask Him.)

He quickly spoke back to me, "Lovers don't yell in one another's ears."

God is so logical. Those in love do not yell at one another. They communicate in gentleness and tenderness. They also communicate by a look in the eyes, a touch, a smile or a whisper. God sees our relationship with Him as based on love. Love does not demand. Love is gentle. Love is kind, but firm (see 1 Corinthians 13).

God Is So Good—and Practical

My appreciation of the Lord's ways has grown over time, as I have realized how much He desires to save us trouble and heartache. When we are seeking Him about something, we need to remind ourselves that He knows the end from the beginning about every situation. He is the Alpha and the Omega—the beginning and the end. He sees a larger picture than we do. What looks good to us may be greatly limited, if not distorted in our eyes.

For example, I asked God why He never released me to speak in certain circles. I knew that the people I was praying about were good people who loved Him, and it did not make sense to me that He did not release me to go to those certain places and people to minister. As I sought Him about this, He spoke the words "different interstates."

The Holy Spirit was simply saying that just as in the natural we can travel on different interstates, in the spiritual some Christians are on a different interstate than others. The callings of God are different, and therefore the vision can be totally different.

On the other hand, how exciting it is to be called to places and be led into fellowship with spiritual cousins—those who have heard the Holy Spirit in similar ways. Young Mary, upon being told by the angel Gabriel that she was the vessel God was using to bring forth Christ, was immediately sent to her cousin Elizabeth. This cousin had also had a supernatural encounter and was carrying John the Baptist in her womb.

The Holy Spirit confirmed their encounter, and Elizabeth's baby leaped in her womb when she heard Mary's salutation: "And it happened, when Elizabeth heard the greeting of Mary, that the babe leaped in her womb; and

Elizabeth was filled with the Holy Spirit" (Luke 1:41). This was indicative of the Holy Spirit bearing witness.

When God births something in your inner being, He will be faithful to give you "cousins" with similar experiences. My advice? Get around people who make your "baby" jump!

We miss out when we try to do God's work on our own initiative. To me, it seems rare to meet an evangelist who prays about where the Lord is actually sending him to minister. It is shameful how some see only open doors and ignore the pure will of the Lord regarding their ministries. But why should we want to minister anywhere, unless we are sent there by the Holy Spirit?

One day the Lord spoke this: "Listening to God is hard on the flesh. It is a discipline that contradicts the soulish (emotional) desires of men."

The flesh recoils at the discipline of listening. It is easier to follow our own inclinations.

Pure Motives

In this same regard, a number of years ago, after the Lord called me to travel full-time as an evangelist, He cautioned me, "Never look at honorariums—look at lives."

Obviously, no minister should be in the ministry for money, but solely because of the call of God. If we will remain concerned about lives and doing the will of God, He will take care of the finances. If God has called us, He will supply. Our part is to pay attention to the Holy Spirit and go where He directs—along with being willing *not* to go when we are not being sent.

God assumes the responsibility for our needs if we pursue Him and obey Him. If it is *our* ministry, it is not worth anything anyway. If it is *His* ministry, He will supply. God is not limited to supplying in a specific way. Again, if we walk in obedience, He will supply through various means. There will be no lack. He is Jehovah-Jireh—the Provider.

Now we have discovered that we can hear God through the Bible and the proceeding word, through His thoughts in our mind, through words of knowledge and through His words in our spirit. In the next chapter we will discover yet another way we can hear Him, as we discuss how the Holy Spirit speaks to us through pictures and visions.

5

Hearing God through Holy Spirit Pictures and Visions

A picture is worth a thousand words.

> I have also spoken by the prophets, and I have
> multiplied visions, and used similitudes, by
> the ministry of the prophets.
>
> Hosea 12:10 KJV

I stood praying for a middle-aged man, Jim, following a Christian men's breakfast. As I prayed, I "saw" him dressed in a military uniform. As I related this to him, he teared up. He told me that when he was a young man he had tried to join the military, but he did not pass the physical.

After the physical he drove home deeply disappointed with the news, but as he pondered it, the Holy Spirit spoke to him: "Don't worry, because I've called you to My army."

Thirty years later, after he had been serving God faithfully, the Holy Spirit reminded him of the day he had been called into the army of God. What I saw and experienced as I prayed for Jim was a picture by the Spirit. Some would say it was a vision, but although it was from the Holy Spirit, it was two-dimensional—more like looking at a photograph. This kind of picture is one of the most common, helpful and practical ways God speaks to us.

In Hosea 12:10, the King James Version uses the word *similitudes*, which is the translation of the Hebrew word *damah*, meaning mental pictures or images. Many prophets of old would see pictures as they prophesied, literally prophesying what they were seeing. Centuries before photography or television, prophetic people were seeing "photographs" and "videos" as they prayed.

Plainly, this is still one of the tools God uses to communicate His mind to His people. I have heard countless Christians with whom I was praying say, "As we were praying, I saw . . ." When the person describes what he or she saw by the Spirit, the picture is vividly and accurately describing the mind of the Lord regarding the situation, or giving wisdom concerning it.

A similitude or picture given by the Spirit could easily be described as an impression someone sees in his or her spirit. When praying, usually with your eyes closed, the Holy Spirit will faithfully begin giving you pictures that portray the answers to what you are praying about. They may be still pictures or moving scenes. Although the pictures (similitudes) are not visions, they are clear.

A true vision is more of a three-dimensional experience. In fact, people usually see visions with their eyes wide open. Again, a picture (similitude) or a mental image is more two-dimensional, almost like looking at a photograph. Most of the Christians I have been around will use the term *vision* when the Lord shows them a picture, but in actuality what they saw was a Holy Spirit picture—a similitude. Whether we refer to it as a vision or a picture (similitude), however, it is from the Lord.

I believe many of the prayers we pray are prophetic prayers, with the words being given to us by the Holy Spirit. Many times it is clear that the prayer being offered is actually equivalent to prophecy, because there is an awareness of the Holy Spirit anointing every word.

Following such prayers, it is not uncommon to hear people comment, "As I was praying, the Lord showed me a picture of . . ." (whatever they see). Then they will describe what they saw as they prayed. There is always satisfaction that comes in knowing the prayer was in the perfect will of God, as people know they were praying exactly what the Spirit was showing them.

Worth a Thousand Words

Why does God speak through pictures? Pictures are not easily forgotten, and they always prove extremely accurate. A picture is worth a thousand words. Many times the pictures that come are almost humorous. For example, you might be praying for a man and seeing God "checking his oil" (spiritually), when in life it turns out that he is a mechanic.

I guess the Lord does this kind of thing to reassure the person we are praying for that He knows him or her. In one city, as I prayed for one man I kept seeing everything having to do with fire, such as that God would start fires in the hearts of people and that He encourages people to be fervent for Him.

Later, that man's pastor said to me, "Do you know what he does for a living? He's a fireman."

One time the Lord drew my attention to a man and I "saw" him with a weak spine, so I asked him, "Do you have back problems?"

"No," he replied.

This really threw me because I knew what I had seen by the Spirit. Later, the pastor confided to me that this man was very spineless and would never use his God-given authority. Then I understood that the Lord was talking about his spiritual back. He needed a backbone.

Jesus was seeing by the Spirit when He met Nathaniel for the first time and said, "Behold an Israelite indeed, in whom is no guile!" (John 1:47 KJV).

Nathaniel was amazed and asked Him, "How do You know me?"

Jesus answered and said to him, "Before Philip called you, when you were under the fig tree, I saw you" (John 1:48).

All of us need to know that God notices us. Sure, we can get to heaven without such experiences, but it is just like the sweet Holy Spirit to encourage us on earth. He is the "God of all comfort" (2 Corinthians 1:3).

I have known Mike for many years. He had once been an excellent car body man, but it was while working in this occupation that he contracted lupus because of the paint fumes. The lupus ultimately destroyed his kidneys, and he underwent a kidney transplant. Now, twenty years later, Mike has been through years of struggles, yet his attitude is extremely positive. He ministers to more people than anyone I know.

One night I was speaking in the church Mike attends in Tennessee. After preaching, I was praying for various people and felt prompted of the Spirit to pray for him. People love Mike, and everyone was interested. As I began to pray, I expressed out loud what the Holy Spirit was showing me.

"Mike," I said, "I see you like an older car with a lot of dents and dings, and the paint looks a little rough, but this car is still good for many miles."

Everyone's laughter showed their affection for Mike and how much they appreciated the Lord's promise to him. That has been a number of years ago, and although Mike still struggles with health issues, he continues to live today.

Sweet Holy Spirit

There is a sweetness about the Holy Spirit that words cannot describe. He is the Comforter, the Encourager, the Helper. I like to refer to Him as user-friendly and as a sweetheart. Think about His nature; think about the fruit of the Spirit. All fruit is sweet. All aspects of His character are sweet. Even as I retell some of these experiences of how He encourages people, letting them know how intimately interested He is in their lives, I stand amazed.

While speaking in a church in Kentucky, right at the very end of the meeting the Holy Spirit drew me to a couple on the front row. I did not know they were first-time visitors and that they had never been to this church (or any church like it). I was especially drawn to the wife.

Feeling great compassion, I prayed for her gently, telling her three words I saw: "No more disappointments."

Tears began to stream down her face in response. After the meeting, the friend who had invited the couple told me their story. Recently, their one-year-old infant son, who was in perfect health, had contracted spinal meningitis and had died within a few days. That night I met them, they had come to church to seek answers.

God is so good. Nearly two years later when traveling to that city, I saw the couple again. The Lord had blessed them with another son.

More About Similitudes

Through the years, God has spoken to me through pictures (similitudes) more than any other way. Although they come most frequently when I am praying with my eyes closed, sometimes I will see them while in conversation or while speaking prophetically, or even while preaching. These pictures are extremely accurate. Without fail, they always describe either the situation I am praying about or the circumstances in the life of the person about whom I am prophesying.

Seeing a similitude or picture is similar to looking at a photograph or recalling a vivid memory of something. It is as though you can look inside your inner man momentarily. There is no question that seeing this way by the Spirit is seeing into the realm of the spirit world. I rarely experience any sensation or supernatural feeling when it happens. In fact, it seems natural and easy. It is easy because it comes by the Spirit, not by the effort of the flesh.

Frequently, when I am praying about decisions, the Lord will give me these pictures by the Holy Spirit. For example, when I ask the Lord if I am to accept an invitation to a certain city, He may speak by showing me a picture regarding whether or not this is indeed His will. The meaning of the picture given by the Spirit is usually obvious enough so that there will be no strain in interpreting it.

When I was praying about an investment one time, the Lord

revealed a picture through the Spirit of a water sprinkler, but the water was coming out in a weak stream. The Lord was saying that the investment was not promising, but was mediocre. Had the picture been of water coming out forcefully, I would have concluded that it was a good investment. The investment proved mediocre indeed, with minimal results, proving the accuracy of the similitude.

It is always important to pray for the interpretation of similitudes given by the Spirit. Usually, however, what the Lord is saying is plain and graphic. The Holy Spirit is faithful to give us understanding.

One time I was praying for a friend of mine who lives in another city. The Spirit gave me a picture of him walking on stilts. I was drawn to how the stilts made him tower over everything around him. I shared this similitude from the Lord with him. Two months later, he called to tell me that after I had shared with him, he went through several trying circumstances—a death in the family, a situation in his business and so forth. During this time of hardship, however, he was reminded of the picture the Holy Spirit gave me of him on stilts, and he knew that the Lord was reminding him to stay above the situations.

Another time I was flattered by an invitation to speak at a large gathering, and I began to pray about it. In prayer, the Lord revealed a picture of a cruet that contained a slight amount of oil. He also revealed a picture of a large mailbox with only a few letters inside. Both pictures clearly represented minimal results. The oil (a move of the Spirit) would be very little, and the letters in the mailbox (messages from the Spirit) would be limited, without freedom to come forth. The Lord was saying there would be little benefit to going, so I declined the invitation.

Other times when I pray about whether to accept invitations, the Spirit has revealed encouraging things such as abundant fruit or a rushing river (the Holy Spirit). Or He may make known to me that in the place I am asking about, the people are very hungry for the moving of the Holy Spirit.

Whatever the case, God is practical. As He speaks in this way, it is hard to misinterpret what He is saying. The times I have failed to hear correctly and have accepted an invitation I should have declined, I felt as though I was ministering under my own initiative, and the fruit was minimal. I have had to learn to listen carefully to the Holy Spirit. He does not lie, and He knows the hearts of people and whether they will be receptive. What an awesome God we serve! How exciting and amazing it is to realize He can be so intimate and so specific in speaking to His people.

A pastor of a prominent church called me for prayer concerning his wife's physical condition. She had just been diagnosed with a serious ailment. I had already heard about his wife's condition through someone else, and I had sought the Lord concerning her. In prayer I saw in the Spirit a picture of a clump of deep-rooted weeds being pulled up easily. So when this pastor called, I told him what the Lord had revealed—that the condition would be taken care of easily. To their relief, within a week the medical report came back stating that the problem had reversed itself and that she would be fine. God does not lie.

Visions

A few months ago, I was the guest minister at a missionary training school in Illinois. My speaking schedule covered five days, with both morning and evening meetings. After the second day I was feeling a little weak, so after the morning meeting I thought I would take a short nap. As I awoke from the nap and sat up, there was a tarantula on my bed. I swung my hand to knock it off the bed, but there was nothing there. Yet I had seen it vividly with my eyes wide open!

The following three days I was under attack physically, sometimes wondering how I would make it through the next meeting. I was weak, but the Lord sustained me and it ended up being a wonderful week. I knew the vision of the tarantula was a vision simply showing me I was under attack. I will never forget how real that spider appeared.

It seems that seeing an actual vision is a far more rare occurrence than seeing pictures. A vision is an extremely vivid experience. The Lord lifts a veil momentarily to reveal something. The person seeing the vision may well see it with eyes wide open. In fact, a vision will be so real that it appears as real life.

A number of years ago, I awoke one morning and, with my eyes wide open, literally saw a vision of a book I had previously read. The book was *Spiritual Authority* by Watchman Nee. Instantly, along with the vision of the book came a clear knowledge that I was to give the book to a certain pastor. I sent it to him and received word back later that he had been teaching on the subject at the time and was seeking God on the matter. He was greatly encouraged by getting the book, and it had a strong impact on his ministry.

Again, I believe that a vision is a rare occurrence, while seeing a picture (similitude) may be a daily experience. But whether you see a picture or a vision, the bottom line is that it is the voice of God.

The Bible is full of references to visions. Paul had a vision about Ananias: "And in a vision he has seen a man named

Ananias coming in and putting his hand on him, so that he might receive his sight" (Acts 9:12).

Cornelius was given a vision to "connect" with Peter: "About the ninth hour of the day he saw clearly in a vision an angel of God coming in and saying to him, 'Cornelius!'" (Acts 10:3).

Then Peter had a vision as well, "and saw heaven opened and an object like a great sheet bound at the four corners, descending to him and let down to the earth" (verse 11).

It is safe to say that the Holy Spirit has always communicated in this way.

What to Do with It?

It is one thing to receive something from God; it is another thing to know what to do with it. First of all, it is always safe to take the spiritual approach. Look at anything He says as having a spiritual meaning. For example, dreams about giving birth (although they could be literal) usually mean God is birthing something new in your life. Dreams about death usually mean death to self-will. I will discuss more about symbols and their meanings in the next chapter, which is about dreams. Always pray for the interpretation of a picture or a vision. I assure you, interpretation will come much easier as you have more experiences in hearing God in these ways.

Since "God is Spirit" (John 4:24), He speaks in spiritual terms. This is where people get confused. His voice is spiritual, visions are spiritual and dreams are spiritual. If we try to bring spiritual things down to a natural level, nothing makes sense. "Now we have received, not the spirit of the world, but the Spirit who is from God, that we might *know* the things that have been freely given to us by God" (1 Corinthians 2:12, emphasis added).

To understand what God is giving us by His Spirit, we must have spiritual understanding. Anything received from the Spirit (words, dreams, visions, etc.) needs spiritual interpretation. It is important to pray for interpretation and let the *same* Holy Spirit who gave it to you interpret it for you. "These things we also speak, not in words which man's wisdom teaches but which the Holy Spirit teaches, comparing spiritual things with spiritual" (1 Corinthians 2:13).

Now we have talked about hearing God through the Bible and the proceeding word, through His thoughts, words of knowledge and His words in our spirit. We have also talked about hearing Him through pictures and visions. In the next chapter, let's look at yet another way God speaks to us—through dreams.

6

Hearing God through Dreams

The prophet who has a dream, let him tell
a dream.

Jeremiah 23:28

It was a privilege to start my first and only pastorate in Beaumont, Texas, but after eight years I was experiencing a lot of unrest and dissatisfaction. Pastoring was a wonderful experience in many ways, but I sensed the Lord had something else in mind for me.

The dissatisfaction seemed to intensify more and more, until one night I had a dream. In the dream, I was standing on the very top of the Empire State Building. The dream was so vivid that I could feel the building swaying under my feet. A man to the side of me jumped off the building. Firemen below were holding a net, but he missed it and fell to his death.

Then I heard the voice of the Lord say, "Now it's your turn."

Fearful of jumping, I said, "Where is the elevator?"

Immediately a security guard appeared and took me to an elevator. We got on the elevator, and it went down two floors and stopped. The doors opened and there was a crowd of extremely obese people in front of me. I knew that there was no way for me to proceed. I told the security guard to take me back to the top of the building.

When we arrived, the voice of the Lord spoke again: "I want you to leave your comfortable place and take a giant leap of faith."

Instantly I awoke and knew the interpretation of the dream. Clearly, God was instructing and directing me to step out in faith and resign my pastorate. I knew the extremely obese people represented the path of the flesh, and if I followed the security of the flesh, my destiny would go nowhere.

The following Sunday I stood before the people, told them my experience and resigned, turning the church over to my associates. Since that time, the Lord has graciously opened doors for me to travel and speak to the Body of Christ at large. I have been privileged to visit many countries.

God promised that He would speak to His people through prophecy, visions and dreams in the last days:

> And it shall come to pass in the last days, says God, that I will pour out of My Spirit on all flesh; your sons and your daughters shall prophesy, your young men shall see visions, your old men shall dream dreams.
>
> Acts 2:17

It is important to notice that as soon as the Scripture talks about God pouring out His Spirit, it is immediately followed by, "Your sons and your daughters shall prophecy, your young men shall see visions, your old men shall dream dreams." In other words, when the Spirit moves, God is talking.

God gives dreams for direction, encouragement and comfort. He also gives dreams as warnings, instruction and correction. And some dreams are simply prophetic, telling of things to come.

Praying for several people one Sunday evening in Tennessee, I knew as I prayed for a certain lady that she had been greatly influenced by her father. As I related this to her, she told me that her father had been a great man of God and had died recently. The night of his death, she had a dream that her dad had given her his shoes. I immediately knew what the Lord was saying—He (and her dad) wanted her to walk in his footsteps.

Old Testament Dreams

God has always spoken through dreams. In Jeremiah 23:28, He says, "The prophet who has a dream, let him tell a dream; and he who has My word, let him speak My word faithfully." Job 33:15 tells us, "In a dream, in a vision of the night, when deep sleep falls upon men, while slumbering on their beds, then He opens the ears of men, and seals their instruction."

Joseph had two dreams in which his brothers were bowing down to him, but he did not use much wisdom in letting them know about the dreams:

> Now Joseph had a dream, and he told it to his brothers; and they hated him even more. So he said to them, "Please hear this dream which I have dreamed: There we were, binding sheaves in the field. Then behold, my sheaf arose and also

stood upright; and indeed your sheaves stood all around and bowed down to my sheaf."

. . . Then he dreamed still another dream and told it to his brothers, and said, "Look, I have dreamed another dream. And this time, the sun, the moon, and the eleven stars bowed down to me."

Genesis 37:5–7, 9

Abimelech was warned in a dream regarding Abraham's wife, Sarah. God called him a dead man if he did not restore her to Abraham (see Genesis 20).

Daniel (Belteshazzar) not only had to interpret King Nebuchadnezzar's dream, but he had to tell what it was the king had dreamed (see Daniel 2:26–45).

"At Gibeon the Lord appeared to Solomon in a dream by night; and God said, 'Ask! What shall I give you?'" (1 Kings 3:5).

Jacob dreamed and saw a ladder going up into heaven (see Genesis 28:10–12). Jacob was also given specific direction about his inheritance in a dream (see Genesis 31:10–13).

Ask the Lord for Dreams

Let me encourage you to ask the Lord to speak to you in dreams. God commands us to ask, seek and knock (see Luke 11:9–13). Dreams are a way the Holy Spirit will speak to us.

Over the years, I have had many dreams. In fact, I rarely go to bed without asking God to speak to me through a dream—whether it is for encouragement, learning, direction or correction. I always have a paper and pen handy to write down my dreams. If God knows the number of hairs on our head, He is not limited in speaking to us through dreams. Ask!

Let's look more closely at the different kinds of dreams the Holy Spirit gives to us.

Dreams of Direction

In the New Testament, people were given a number of dreams. Some were for direction. Think about the dreams that came surrounding Jesus' birth. After Mary had conceived by the Holy Spirit, God spoke to Joseph in a dream, directing him and comforting him (see Matthew 1:18–21). Joseph also had two more dreams of direction, one about taking Mary and the child into Egypt to escape Herod, and another about returning to Israel when it was safe (see Matthew 2). The wise men who came bearing gifts for Jesus were warned in a dream not to return to Herod, so they went back to their country by another route (see Matthew 2:12).

Dreams of Warning

Some dreams came as warnings. Pilot's wife was warned in a dream about her husband's dealings with Jesus: "While he was sitting on the judgment seat, his wife sent to him, saying, 'Have nothing to do with that just Man, for I have suffered many things today in a dream because of Him'" (Matthew 27:19).

When I was a pastor, I had a warning dream. I had convinced my church board that we were to purchase a piece of property adjacent to the church. We were excited. The contract offer was signed and we were getting ready to do the final legwork. Then one night, the Lord spoke to me in a dream that I was not in His will buying the property. This caught me by surprise, but the dream was so very clear that I instantly obeyed. I repented to the Lord and to the board members for acting in presumption and emotion instead of in the mind of the Spirit.

Dreams of Encouragement and Comfort

Other dreams are given for encouragement and comfort. Some close friends of ours lost their young son through a tragic drowning accident. Later, the grief-stricken mother became pregnant. Several weeks before the child was born, I had a dream that she gave birth to a boy. Around that same time, her husband called to tell me about his dream, which was almost identical to mine. In it, his wife had given birth to a baby boy.

Weeks passed and the baby was born, but it was a girl. My friend was disappointed and angry at God because we had both dreamed that the child would be a boy. Then it became apparent that God was speaking about a child yet to come. God obviously knew that the first child would be a girl and that the young father would be disappointed, so He gave us both dreams about them having a son as an encouragement.

When his wife conceived again, this time she gave birth to a son. Even the parents recognized not only God's comfort, but His wisdom in giving them the son as the second child. If the son had come first, they would have been tempted to expect him to replace the son who had drowned. But the way God ordered the births, both children wound up being a tremendous blessing to this godly couple.

Dreams of Instruction

Some dreams are given for instruction. Recently I had a dream that I was flying a small Cessna, a one-engine plane. Jesus was seated next to me, but He was not observing my flying ability. Rather, He was casually reading something. As I piloted the plane, I continued to fly perilously close to the tops of trees and telephone wires. Several times I abruptly pulled up just before nearly hitting something. Finally we landed, to my great relief.

As I awoke from the dream, I immediately knew the interpretation. God was telling me I could "fly higher" in the Spirit. I did not have to fly so near the earth. Jesus' nonchalant attitude as He sat with me in the plane was indicative of God letting it be *my* choice how high I wanted to live in the Spirit. The dream was not only for instruction, but was a sweet rebuke to live more in the Spirit and to stop letting natural circumstances (nearly hitting trees, etc.) influence my life.

Dreams of Correction

Some dreams provide correction. In my senior year of college, I was involved in the leadership of a sovereign move of the Holy Spirit on the University of Nebraska campus. Every Tuesday night scores of students would pour into the campus chapel, where we would worship and let the Holy Spirit move among us. Many students came to know the Lord and were baptized in the Holy Spirit.

God was wooing these young people to Himself, and one newly born-again coed related a dream she had to me. In her dream, the Holy Spirit was talking to her and telling her to choose between her boyfriend and me. When she related the dream, she already knew the interpretation and knew that I represented the Lord in the dream. He was telling her to choose between her boyfriend (who would lead her more deeply into the world) and the Lord.

Quite often in dreams, those in leadership capacities represent the Lord Himself. Sometimes a person's father (who may not even be living) will represent God the Father in the dream.

I have had a number of dreams where I was involved in a heated battle. In one dream, I was having a heated argument with someone. The following day I faced a tremendous temptation, but when the opportunity presented itself, I immediately remembered the dream. I knew that the argument represented a battle with my flesh, and it brought encouragement and strength for me to resist the temptation and win the battle. It is important to realize that often in dreams people are representative of other things, and God may not be talking to us about the actual person who appears in the dream.

On another occasion, I was striving (as many preachers do) to get a message to preach for an upcoming meeting. Nothing came alive out of the Word and I began to feel impatient, until I looked through my bookshelf and found a small booklet by the late E. W. Kenyon. As I began to read it, I got excited about the truth in it and began to take notes verbatim, until I had a complete teaching. Since I had gained many new understandings from what I read, I decided to teach on that subject the following day.

That night, God spoke to me through a dream in which I was in a grocery store. I walked over to the fruit display, grabbed a banana, peeled it and began to eat it. Suddenly the store manager came out of nowhere and said to me, "You're going to have to pay for that!"

I immediately awakened from the dream and knew the interpretation. The store manager was the Lord. I was "stealing" food that I had found in Mr. Kenyon's book. I was getting ready to preach another man's revelation, which was a result of his efforts to seek God, not my efforts. Obviously, the Lord was not pleased with my decision to preach another man's revelation. I would have been giving leftovers to the people rather than something fresh from God's "griddle." I immediately received God's correction and repented.

Prophetic Dreams

God also gives us dreams that are prophetic. It is like receiving a prophecy in your sleep. One night during my college years, I had a dream that I was giving birth to a baby. I could literally feel the birth pangs and was in a hospital delivery room, going through the whole process, until the baby came.

As I awoke from the dream (which was so real), I promised myself that I would never tell anyone that dream. Then a few days later, at 11:00 p.m. one night, there was a knock on my window. My good friend from high school wanted to talk to me. He had just had a big fight with his girlfriend. As we talked for the next two hours, I led him to Christ (and he is a Christian to this day). A few days later, it suddenly hit me—I did indeed have a baby! I had led my friend to Christ.

Interpreting Dreams and Visions

Dream interpretation becomes easy when you do not try to interpret dreams through your brain. To strain through logic and reasoning to understand the meaning of a dream or vision is an exercise in futility. The interpretation of a dream only comes by revelation of the Spirit.

It will also be helpful to you to become familiar with the symbols I list in the next section that represent various things in dreams. These symbols have stood the test of time and make interpreting dreams much easier. We will get to those in a moment, but first, here are four important keys to dream interpretation that will also help you.

1. Interpret by the Spirit

In the beginning, I could not seem to catch the meaning of dreams, until I became aware of seeing them through spiritual eyes. If an interpretation does not come readily, do not strive with it. Simply put the dream on the shelf. God is well able to bring us illumination. He knows how our analytical minds tend to stand in the way, so He will "drop in" the interpretation of the dream at an unexpected time—a time when we are not striving over it.

2. Always Keep It Simple

The Holy Spirit never complicates things. In fact, He simplifies them. If interpreting a dream is complicated and confusing, you are not hearing the Holy Spirit. Either that, or you may be attempting to gain interpretation through your carnal mind. Again, the Lord will be faithful to give you understanding and interpretation. It is also okay to share a dream with someone who walks with the Lord. Often, that person will recognize something you did not and be able to provide insight into the interpretation.

3. Figurative or Literal?

Sometimes God is speaking figuratively, and other times He is speaking literally. We must discern the difference. Some people receive dreams that provide specific direction about what to do, such as buying a certain piece of property. Other times, a similar dream may be God speaking spiritually, and a piece of property could simply represent increasing the Kingdom of God. A father, pastor or other leader usually represents the Lord in dreams. Children can represent baby Christians. Again, the same Holy Spirit who gives the dream will supply the interpretation and show you whether the dream is figurative or literal. Remember that symbols are common in dreams.

4. Do Not Get Mystical or Super-Religious

God is practical and gives us dreams, visions and encouragement meant to help us in our everyday lives. Some people spiritualize things to such an extreme that they are far removed from reality. If we become overly mystical, it alienates and frightens others from receiving the things of God. We need to stay rooted in reality.

Colors and Other Symbols

Many people ask about the meaning of colors and other symbols that appear in dreams. The Holy Spirit will often use colors and symbols in dreams and visions to emphasize a truth. Here are a few symbolisms I have learned through many years of experience with this area:

- *Red* represents the power of salvation and the blood of Jesus.
- *White* represents the Holy Spirit and the purity of the Holy Spirit.
- *Green* represents peace. "He makes me to lie down in green pastures" (Psalm 23:2).
- *Blue* represents the depth of the Holy Spirit. When you look at water or the sky in depth, they appear blue.
- *Purple* represents the Kingdom of God—royalty.
- *Pink* represents the working power of the Holy Spirit. Pink is a mixture of red (salvation power) and white (the Holy Spirit).
- *Yellow* represents joy—sunlight.

- *Water* represents a type of the Holy Spirit.

    Still water represents peace or calm.

    Moving water represents the flow of the Holy Spirit.

    Stagnant water represents the lack of moving of the Holy Spirit.

    Dirty water represents spirit mixed with flesh.

- *Mud* and *dirt* are indicative of the flesh.

- *Wood* represents flesh (wood, hay and straw; see 1 Corinthians 3:12).

- *Fire* represents the consuming power of the Holy Spirit (see Matthew 3:12).

- *Guns* usually represent authority, unless you are in the context of being shot at by evil people.

- *Police* and *judiciary people* represent the law.

- *Feet* or *shoes* represent the spiritual walk.

- *Hands* represent ministry.

- The *back* or *backbone* represents strength or steadfastness.

- The *nose* represents discernment and discerning good or evil (i.e., foul odors or pleasant aromas).

- The *neck* speaks of yieldedness to God's direction. The neck turns the head. Scripture speaks of the stiff-necked and those who bow the neck.

- *Animals,* especially *dogs, cats* and *cows,* represent the flesh, and a *skunk* represents an evil spirit.

- A *hoodlum* (or a dark-hooded individual) usually represents an evil spirit.

- *Hair* represents the glory of God.

    Often *black hair* represents youth and strength.

    White hair represents wisdom.

    Red hair represents a child of God.

Blond hair also represents a child of God in the sense of youth and vibrancy.

- *Leaders, ministers, doctors* and *fathers* often represent the Lord.

It is important to note that many of these symbolisms are not absolute, but they can serve as helpful guidelines. Each person must pray and ask the Lord for a dream's interpretation. The same Holy Spirit who gives the dream or vision desires to give the interpretation. Although it is not wrong to seek counsel if you need help with an interpretation, I believe the Holy Spirit desires to give the interpretation to the same person to whom He gave the picture, dream or vision.

There is also the danger of twisting the meaning of a dream or vision around to something other than what God intended. When people harden their hearts, although God is trying to speak to them, they "interpret" every dream or vision to mean something it does not. With some people who have told me their dreams, it was obvious to me that God was trying to bring them correction, but they had twisted the interpretation around to mean something totally different.

We have to be careful to maintain a teachable spirit when we are dealing with this area (or any other). And we have to be careful not to try to help God out by attempting to bring a dream to pass ourselves. We need to pray about it, welcome the Holy Spirit daily and stay focused on what He has shown us.

Now we have seen several amazing ways in which we can hear the voice of God—through the written Word and the proceeding word, through God's thoughts in our mind, through words of knowledge, through God's words in our spirit, through Holy Spirit pictures and visions, and through dreams. Let's look in the next chapter at another amazing way to hear God that we can add to this list—how the Holy Spirit lets us hear His voice through His peace.

7

Hearing God through His Peace

Let the peace of God rule in your hearts.

Colossians 3:15

The peace of God is a priceless benefit in our relationship with the Lord. Sometimes I wonder if we take it for granted. God's peace is that internal tranquilizer that governs our being. Jesus promised us peace: "Peace I leave with you, My peace I give to you; not as the world gives do I give to you. Let not your heart be troubled, neither let it be afraid" (John 14:27).

One way God talks to us is through His peace, or sometimes through our sensing a lack of peace. The first thing we need to recognize in order to clearly hear Him this way is that there is a difference between having the peace *of* God and having peace *with* God.

Certainly any born-again believer who loves God and desires to serve Him has peace *with* God. This is simply part of the blood covenant. His peace is part of the package. Romans 5:1 says, "Therefore, having been justified by faith, we have peace with God through our Lord Jesus Christ." Ephesians 2:13–14 tells us, "But now in Christ Jesus you who once were far off have been brought near by the blood of Christ. For He Himself is our peace, who has made both one, and has broken down the middle wall of separation."

Sensing the peace *of* God (or a lack of that peace) is one of the undeniable ways He speaks to believers in specific situations. This is best made clear where Paul tells us God's peace acts like an umpire:

> And let the peace (soul harmony which comes) from Christ rule (*act as an umpire continually*) in your hearts [deciding and settling with finality all questions that arise in your minds, in that peaceful state] to which as [members of Christ's] one body you were also called [to live]. And be thankful (appreciative), [giving praise to God always].
>
> Colossians 3:15 AMPLIFIED, emphasis added

The Holy Spirit within us is that heavenly umpire who continually declares peace . . . or a lack of peace.

When a Christian expresses concerning some decision, "I just don't have peace about it," that person is not saying he or she does not have peace *with* God. Rather, the person is saying there is a lack of the peace *of* God concerning that specific decision.

At other times, when a decision has to be made, the Holy Spirit within may give a believer a tremendous inundation of peace (like a double dose) that gives assurance. This overwhelming peace is an indication that the decision is in the will of God. The peace is so overwhelming that it is hard to resist a smile or even laughter, and it carries a sense of extreme assurance.

When encountering difficult circumstances, you may feel as though you are in a dark tunnel. Feelings of hopelessness can flood your soul. Yet it is in such situations that the sweet Holy Spirit will begin to minister peace. His peace will invade your being, standing between you and the storm clouds, commanding them to dissipate. This is peace that defies understanding and commands hopelessness to retreat. It overwhelms your spirit: "And the peace of God, which surpasses all understanding, will guard your hearts and minds through Christ Jesus" (Philippians 4:7).

That kind of peace is the voice of God saying loudly, "Fear not! All is well." His peace is His voice. Circumstances become irrelevant because the peace of God has flooded your inner being.

Peace or Counterfeit Peace?

When hearing God through His peace, we do need to discern the difference between peace in our spirit and peace in our soul. There is a difference (see Hebrews 4:12).

The soulish (emotional) part of us can become highly enthusiastic about a decision if it is something we really want to do. If we are not careful, we can wrongly diagnose this euphoria and excitement as God's peace and be deceived into thinking God is giving us an affirmative answer. But it is deep in our spirit where the heavenly umpire will declare peace or refuse to manifest peace.

In situations where our emotions are overly excited, it helps to prayerfully wait upon the Lord for a season before making a decision. This waiting period gives our emotions a chance to cool down. Our emotions can make us feel a counterfeit peace, but waiting on the Lord will clarify things for us because a real peace will remain, while emotions will fade away.

Do not forget that passivity also can look like peace. Without a prayer life, we aimlessly wander through life calling what we have "peace," when actually it is passivity because we have surrendered our zeal to being passive.

Peace as Our Guide

It is so significant that the Lord guides us through peace. It is a common denominator in knowing the will of God. For example, husbands and wives know immediately when communication has broken down between them. Something is lacking; something is missing. One of them might ask the other, "What's wrong?"

Likewise, when we walk with God and begin to turn the wrong way, we may immediately sense something lacking. We know His peace is mysteriously missing. We should be sensitive to that lack of peace and ask, "What's wrong here, Lord?"

Picture yourself on a walk with someone. You are striding along talking, and suddenly you realize the person who was at your side is gone. That person's presence is missing. As you look back, you see that the person has stopped a little way back to look at something. Similarly with God, we can become aware when something is not right. As we walk in the Spirit, we should take note of when His peace is missing and turn around. Then we should ask why. He will reveal the reason.

Many times when someone approaches me for counsel and enthusiastically declares his or her plans, it seems that my peace begins to evaporate. I know then that the Guide within is telling me the person is departing from God's will in the matter he or she is speaking about.

Sometimes we experience a sense as though our heart has fallen into our shoelaces. This is especially true in the process of making a decision. You might begin to experience that sinking feeling—your peace is quickly evaporating. (This is totally different from "buyer's remorse," by the way, which is more of a mental torment.) When the peace of God begins to leave, you experience more of a feeling of disappointing the Holy Spirit.

During the times when I am on the verge of making a wrong decision, it seems as though I am retreating from the Holy Spirit. He is simply saying through that lack of peace, "That is not My will; you are not obeying Me."

Having the peace of God, or sensing the absence of His peace, is the voice of the Lord. Clearly, it is one way He communicates with every child who belongs to Him.

So far, we have seen that God talks to us through His Word and proceeding words, through His thoughts, words of knowledge, His words in our spirit, pictures, visions, dreams and peace (or a lack of peace). God also talks to us through the inner witness of His Spirit, which every believer should experience. That inner witness is the topic of the next chapter.

8

Hearing God through the Inner Witness

The Spirit Himself bears witness with our spirit.

Romans 8:16

I have been in situations in which people are telling me the direction they are sensing from the Lord, and as they are telling me, it is as though my spirit is jumping up and down and doing cartwheels in response. I am convinced that the Holy Spirit is simply bearing witness in my spirit to the action they are taking.

Other times, my experience is just the opposite. As people are telling me about a decision they are making, I feel dead and lifeless inside, which makes me aware that the Holy Spirit is not in agreement with them.

Frequently Christians refer to "receiving a witness" about

something they have heard spoken, preached or suggested. But what is a witness of the Spirit? Scripture talks about the Spirit bearing witness: "The Spirit Himself bears witness with our spirit that we are children of God" (Romans 8:16).

In other words, what proof do you have that you are a Christian? Yes, you have the Word of God that says so, but you also have a witness in your heart—a knowing from God Himself. This witness is undeniable and equips you with security and a certainty that you belong to Him.

When someone receives a witness about a step he or she is taking, that person is declaring that they have a "knowing" or a spiritual connection with God inside, and in effect, it is resounding a positive "yes" within. We know that the Holy Spirit is the Spirit of Truth, and He will *always* bear witness to truth. Since He dwells within the believer, He will bear witness to truth in the spirit of the believer. God guides us in our human spirit, which has been made alive through the Holy Spirit.

Proverbs 20:27 says, "The spirit of a man is the lamp of the LORD, searching all the inner depths of his heart." No matter what way the voice of the Lord comes to us, it should always bear witness to our inner man. It is much like a lightbulb turned on in our spirits.

Upon being born again, it is the spirit, not the physical person, that has been made new. Obviously, the physical body does not get changed (at least not right now), but the real person (the spirit) is made brand-new. It is through your spirit that God will guide you. That is where He lives.

In a very practical sense, God will teach you how to recognize an inner witness of truth. First of all, He will never contradict Scripture. Thank God for the written Word, because it is a safeguard against heresy and against those who claim they have heard God and are running with some "new" doctrine.

Second, the Holy Spirit will cause you to have a "knowing" in your spirit when there is a witness or a lack thereof. Each person may experience this in a slightly different way. There is definitely such a thing as a positive or negative witness, and over time believers should develop a sensitivity to those.

One of the most basic ways the Holy Spirit gives witness is His "coming alive" in your spirit. This can be described as a tremendous lightness or a flooding of peace in your inner being. Or in your case, there could be some other similar sensation you feel and become familiar with.

Of course, that does not mean that any tingling sensation you experience is necessarily a witness of the Spirit. We have to discern between our emotions and the mind of the Spirit. Hebrews 4:12 is a great Scripture that describes this truth: "For the word of God is living and powerful, and sharper than any two-edged sword, piercing even to the division of soul and spirit, and of joints and marrow, and is a discerner of the thoughts and intents of the heart." Learning to recognize this difference between soul and spirit involves knowing God and developing an understanding of His ways.

Just as a believer gains assurance in knowing that he or she is saved and ceases to doubt being truly born again, we can all become more confident in recognizing the Spirit bearing witness in our inner being. Then we will become more sensitive to receive direction from the Lord by the witness or lack of witness we experience.

A Check from the Holy Spirit

Just as often as you hear someone talking about a witness, you might hear people say they received "a check" in their spirit. What is a check from the Holy Spirit? A check would best be described as a caution from the Spirit. Just as the Holy Spirit will bear witness to the truth, He may also indicate a lack of truth and show a caution in someone's spirit. He simply is *not* bearing witness to something. Receiving a check, just like a witness, is the result of familiarity and friendship with the Holy Spirit, which has to be developed in the inner being of the believer.

Another way to describe a check from the Holy Spirit is that instead of a lightness or fire in your inner being about something, you may well feel a sudden heaviness or lack of life. Another way to express it would be sensing a sudden deadness in your spirit, or having a sinking, life-evaporating feeling concerning something you are hearing. The Holy Spirit within you is checking you, in effect saying, "I don't agree with this; it is not truth," or "This is not the way I am leading you."

Again, that does not mean that any negative sensation we feel is necessarily a check. We may be feeling our own boredom at the moment or our disinterest in whatever is being expressed. We have to learn to know the Holy Spirit, and we have to be ruthlessly honest with ourselves.

Peter certainly must have experienced a check when Simon the sorcerer offered money to the disciples for the power of the Holy Spirit:

> And when Simon saw that through the laying on of the apostles' hands the Holy Spirit was given, he offered them money, saying, "Give me this power also, that anyone on whom I lay hands may receive the Holy Spirit."
>
> But Peter said to him, "Your money perish with you, because you thought that the gift of God could be purchased with money! You have neither part nor portion in this matter, for your heart is not right in the sight of God. Repent

therefore of this your wickedness, and pray God if perhaps the thought of your heart may be forgiven you. For I see that you are poisoned by bitterness and bound by iniquity."

Acts 8:18–23

Peter let Simon have it because his request was not pure and did not bear witness. I am glad Peter was not tempted to accept Simon's offer of money. There was nothing in Peter that would allow him to compromise his convictions.

The Urim and the Thummim

In a number of instances in the Old Testament, God spoke through the high priest by way of the Urim and Thummim. This rarely studied method has an amazing correlation to the modern way we understand the inner witness of the Holy Spirit. The Urim and Thummim were contained in a pouch that was placed behind the breastplate of the high priest, strategically close to his heart:

And you shall put in the breastplate of judgment the Urim and the Thummim, and they shall be over Aaron's heart when he goes in before the LORD. So Aaron shall bear the judgment of the children of Israel over his heart before the LORD continually.

Exodus 28:30

This was a way for the priest to receive a "yes" or "no" witness from God. Leviticus 8:8 tells us that when Moses consecrated Aaron to the priesthood, "he put the breastplate on him, and he put the Urim and the Thummim in the breastplate." These two "hidden" pieces would give the answer that the priest sought.

The word *Urim* means lights and perfections, while the

word *Thummim* means truths and completeness. You can see the overall balance in this that goes along with Scriptures such as "true worshipers will worship the Father in spirit and truth" (John 4:23).

It is interesting how the wisdom of God put the two together—the Urim (light) for divine guidance, and the Thummim (truth) for integrity of heart. The Holy Spirit will only bear witness to truth.

First John 5:6 states, "And it is the Spirit who bears witness, because the Spirit is truth." The high priest had in his breast-plate at all times the symbols for Spirit and truth. Whenever there was a need for divine guidance regarding a decision, the priest could peek into the pouch behind the breastplate to see if the Urim glowed. If the glow was present, he knew the Lord was speaking a yes. If there was no glow (inner burning), then he knew God was speaking a no, meaning not to take the action they were inquiring about.

> He [Joshua] shall stand before Eleazar the priest, who shall inquire before the LORD for him by the judgment of the Urim. At his word they shall go out, and at his word they shall come in, both he and all the children of Israel with him—all the congregation.
>
> Numbers 27:21

This is exactly what we do as believers. We become conscious of the inner glow, or that witness of the Spirit inside. We can be aware of the Spirit glowing with a resounding yes, or when there is a lack of glowing or burning, a resounding no. Plainly, this is Spirit-led living, or trusting the inner witness of the Holy Spirit within.

It is easy to see how this correlates to New Covenant believers. We have to live by the inner glow of the Holy Spirit.

When we do not have the inner witness, we have to assume that God is saying no.

Psalm 43:3 (emphasis added) says, "Oh, send out Your *light* and Your *truth!* Let them lead me; let them bring me to Your holy hill." Praise the Lord that His Spirit dwells within us as believers and that He promises to lead us and guide us into all truth.

God leads and guides us in so many ways that we have talked about—through the Bible and proceeding words, through His thoughts, words of knowledge, His words in our spirit, pictures, visions, dreams, peace and the inner witness of His Spirit. Now let's look at His voice leading and guiding us through hearing Him in our conscience.

9

Hearing God in Your Conscience

Let your conscience be your guide.

God has created every human being with a conscience, which equips each of us with an innate sense of knowing right from wrong. The human conscience is a gift from God, but it can become calloused and insensitive if we ignore it.

Our conscience is clearly one of the ways God speaks to us. It does not necessarily involve God speaking directly to us, but if we are living open to Him, our conscience gives Him an opportunity to invade our thinking. It acts as a moral compass.

We can define our conscience as the inner sense we have of what is right or wrong in our conduct and motives. That inner sense can guide us toward right actions, if we let it. For example, I would eat another piece of pie, except my conscience would bother me.

We can override our conscience through daily incidences such as cheating at a game, displaying a poor attitude in traffic, taking too long on lunch break, or giving in to the temptation not to point it out when a clerk gives us too much change. Although these seem like small things, our conscience will warn us about them. We can learn to keep our conscience clear by heeding the small warnings it gives us.

As we grow in the Lord, He holds us to a higher standard. Careless habits we once thought nothing about now convict us in our conscience—God's way of letting us know what is displeasing to Him. Listening to Him through our conscience, we begin to learn about being faithful in the little things. "He who is faithful in what is least is faithful also in much; and he who is unjust in what is least is unjust also in much" (Luke 16:10).

Sometimes our conscience will tug at us and tell us to apologize to someone for something we said or did, and we know that we need to make it right. As Matthew 5:23 says,

> Therefore if you bring your gift to the altar, and there remember that your brother has something against you, leave your gift there before the altar, and go your way. First be reconciled to your brother, and then come and offer your gift.

This tugging we feel can be the voice of the Lord clearly talking to us, using our conscience. It is up to us to listen. That is why Paul declared that some who were born with a working conscience have since had it seared with a hot iron. They have given in to evil so frequently and have hardened their hearts so often that there is no more awareness in them of right or wrong. Paul wrote that those who depart from the faith in the latter days will be found "speaking lies in hypocrisy, having their own conscience seared with a hot iron" (1 Timothy 4:2).

At one point when the children of Israel ignored their conscience, they began to accuse God of killing them:

> And all the children of Israel complained against Moses and Aaron, and the whole congregation said to them, "If only we had died in the land of Egypt! Or if only we had died in this wilderness! Why has the Lord brought us to this land to fall by the sword, that our wives and children should become victims? Would it not be better for us to return to Egypt?" So they said to one another, "Let us select a leader and return to Egypt."
>
> Numbers 14:2–4

Because their present circumstances made them feel uncomfortable, they gave in to anger and panic, and they abandoned their faith and their conscience. Can you imagine that after all the Lord had done for them by parting the Red Sea and burying the entire Egyptian army, they chose to harden their hearts?

As we endeavor to follow the Holy Spirit in our daily lives and keep our heart open toward Him, Scripture gives us wisdom to know how to be a reflection of who God is in us. This is to God's glory. Look what Peter wrote about having a good conscience:

> But sanctify the Lord God in your hearts, and always be ready to give a defense to everyone who asks you a reason for the hope that is in you, with meekness and fear; having a good conscience, that when they defame you as evildoers, those who revile your good conduct in Christ may be ashamed.
>
> 1 Peter 3:15–16

For this is commendable, if because of conscience toward God one endures grief, suffering wrongfully. For what credit is it if, when you are beaten for your faults, you take it patiently? But when you do good and suffer, if you take it patiently, this is commendable before God.

1 Peter 2:19–20

Condemnation or Conviction?

Some people struggle with knowing the difference between condemnation and conviction. The word *condemnation* has to do with accusations from the devil. They usually come in the form of harsh, shameful or guilt-producing thoughts from the enemy. But thankfully, there is no condemnation toward believers in Christ (see Romans 8:1).

Conviction, on the other hand, is when the Holy Spirit is gently telling us that we are doing wrong in our actions or motives. This conviction will often occur in our conscience.

The bottom line is that the devil condemns us, and the Holy Spirit convicts us. The devil drives and accuses us from behind, but the Holy Spirit leads us, going before us. The devil tries to separate us, isolate us to get us into a weakened state. He wants us to think that we are the only person having a particular battle. But 1 Peter 5:8–9 tells us how to handle his attacks:

Be sober, be vigilant; because your adversary the devil walks about like a roaring lion, seeking whom he may devour. Resist him, steadfast in the faith, knowing that the same sufferings are experienced by your brotherhood in the world.

The Lord will gently draw us to Himself and endeavor to get us back on the right track. When His conviction shows us what to change in our behavior and attitude, it softens our heart and graces us with a desire to repent. The result is a new strength inside.

The Spirit of the World

When Jesus confronted the religious leaders regarding the woman caught in adultery, He appealed to their conscience:

> So when they continued asking Him, He raised Himself up and said to them, "He who is without sin among you, let him throw a stone at her first." And again He stooped down and wrote on the ground. Then those who heard it, being convicted by their conscience, went out one by one, beginning with the oldest even to the last. And Jesus was left alone, and the woman standing in the midst.
>
> John 8:7–9

In today's society, the powers of darkness work feverishly to get people to ignore their conscience—to ignore their sense of right and wrong. Political correctness is the greatest factor in this, combined with fear of what people think. We are so afraid of offending some special interest group that we cease standing up for truth.

Remember when Elijah was discouraged, thinking he was the only one left standing up for righteousness? But God quickly reminded him that not everyone had crumpled under political pressure: "Yet I have left me seven thousand in Israel, all the knees which have not bowed unto Baal, and every mouth which hath not kissed him" (1 Kings 19:18 KJV).

"Kissing Baal" means surrendering to political correctness. This attitude of compromise is rooted in fear. Often, it is easier to agree with the public view (even when we personally do not support it) than to take a stand. But to surrender and kiss Baal, we have to ignore our conscience.

The spirit of the world wants there to be no absolutes. It wants all of society to tolerate every kind of sin. But tolerating the spirit of this world means ignoring our conscience and taking the easy road.

God will not tolerate that in us, as He told one of the churches in Revelation 2: "Nevertheless I have a few things against you, because you allow that woman Jezebel, who calls herself a prophetess, to teach and seduce My servants to commit sexual immorality and eat things sacrificed to idols" (verse 20).

We cannot tolerate sin and political correctness and get away with it in the Kingdom. We can try to ignore our conscience, but eventually that results in a seared conscience and a hardened heart. It is better to take heed to our conscience and hear what the voice of the Lord is telling us through it. He will speak clearly through our conscience—we just need to listen.

Now that we have taken a close look at several ways in which we can hear the voice of God, in the next chapter we will change direction a little and look at the need to come boldly before His throne.

10

The Need to Come Boldly

Let us therefore come boldly to the throne
of grace.

Hebrews 4:16

It was my first experience speaking at this Texas church.
The church was barely two years old and was meeting in an
elementary school. It was a Sunday morning and the service
had to finish up by noon, which only gave me thirty minutes.
About 180 people were present. I preached briefly, and then
suddenly I was filled with an unusual boldness (maybe because I had so little time).

Looking over at the pastor, I heard myself speaking prophetically to him: "The Lord is going to make a piece of
land available for you. It will be very reasonably priced. The
land will be L-shaped, and this will all happen before your
birthday."

I was amazed at the words coming out of me. Then I began to question myself, thinking, *Did I make this whole thing up?*

Following the meeting, I asked the pastor when his birthday was. He told me the date—only eight weeks away. Now I was really questioning myself, but I have learned that we can trust the Holy Spirit.

Eight weeks later, just one day before the pastor's birthday, he received a call from an elderly man who had heard that the church was looking for a piece of land. This man expressed his desire that the land he owned would be used for the Kingdom of God. He was willing to make his highly coveted property available to the church at a very reasonable price.

To the pastor's amazement, the property was indeed L-shaped and was located along one of the most prominent interstates in the United States. The location was perfect, and the land surrounding the church's new property was in high demand since corporations were building there.

The prophetic words I spoke that day in Texas brought into existence something that might not have happened otherwise. God wants to manifest Himself in our lives in such ways. He wants us to shake off inferiority and unworthiness and boldly declare what He is telling us. The Holy Spirit will speak through any of us. He has good news to tell us, and He desires to give us daily bread—fresh bread—in the form of breaking news.

It is a great thing to enjoy the daily news, but how stale that news becomes a day or two later. No one wants to hear old news. We live in a society of news junkies; we love breaking news. Some television news programs not only tell us the news, but also have a scroll at the bottom of the screen, telling us even more breaking news. This seems like overkill to me. But who wants to hear the same news over and over?

Who has an appetite for old news? When it comes to breaking news, don't you long to hear more than what is on television or in the newspapers? Don't you want to hear what is being served fresh from the "oven" of heaven, too?

A Missing Ingredient

You have been made worthy, so come boldly to God's throne for fresh daily bread. Boldness is a missing ingredient in many lives. Many believers struggle with such unworthiness and low self-worth that they cannot imagine God saying anything to them. But the good news of the Gospel is that as believers, we are worthy and righteous—we just did not have anything to do with it! God did it for us. We did not get here on our own, but we can enjoy what He has accomplished for us.

To hear from God, knowing we are bona fide sons and daughters is key. If we do not understand that we are coming to Him based on His righteousness, we will pray unconvinced, as double-minded people. Religious teaching, combined with the devil's strategy, has convinced many Christians that they are unworthy and undeserving, so God would never speak to them. Yet we are worthy for one reason, that He has forgiven our sins and called us into relationship with Him:

> "This is the covenant that I will make with them after those days, says the LORD: I will put My laws into their hearts, and in their minds I will write them," then He adds, "Their sins and their lawless deeds I will remember no more." Now where there is remission of these, there is no longer an offering for sin.
>
> Therefore, brethren, having boldness to enter the Holiest by the blood of Jesus . . . let us draw near with a true heart in full assurance of faith.
>
> Hebrews 10:16–19, 22

Notice how it says, "I will put My laws in their mind and write them on their hearts." It does not say, "I will put My laws in their Bibles and their notebooks." God is intimate with us. He writes His understanding on our hearts. He has already written His will and His purpose on your heart. It is written in your spiritual DNA.

When I was a boy, I always had a desire to travel. I dreamed of it. Now I have traveled all over the world. People ask me how I can travel so much. I love it and have grace to sleep in different beds every few days. If fact, if I am home for very long, I become anxious to travel somewhere. God wrote it on my heart. Matthew 11:30 says His yoke is easy and His burden is light. His yoke is easy if we are doing what He has yoked us to.

Not an Option

We come boldly because we are forgiven and loved. A lack of boldness is not an option for the believer. "The wicked flee when no one pursues, but the righteous are bold as a lion" (Proverbs 28:1).

I learned boldness from my children. When they were outside and wanted to come inside by way of the front door (which was often locked), they did not gingerly ring the doorbell. They laid on it, making it ring again and again. They were bold because they knew they belonged in the family and had a right of access to any door of the house. Neither did our children ever worry about the status of our bank account. They assumed we had an endless supply.

We must approach God in the same manner. We must be drenched with confidence that we belong to the family of God and that we can boldly access the Holy Spirit. Again, we can come boldly before His throne because He has chosen not to remember our sins. We can come boldly because we are loved. "Love has been perfected among us in this: that we may have boldness in the day of judgment; because as He is, so are we in this world" (1 John 4:17). We can come boldly because He has already lived sinless before us:

> For we do not have a High Priest who cannot sympathize with our weaknesses, but was in all points tempted as we are, yet without sin. Let us therefore come boldly to the throne of grace, that we may obtain mercy and find grace to help in time of need.
>
> Hebrews 4:15–16

If Jesus has paid it all, why are we striving? Here is a Scripture that has been life-changing for me: "And I, if I am lifted up from the earth, will draw all peoples to Myself" (John 12:32). In most translations, this Scripture reads "all peoples" or "all men," but those phrases are added by the translators. In actuality He is saying, "I will draw *all* to Myself." In other words, He took it all to Himself . . . all sin, all wrath, all vengeance, all punishment.

Jesus paid it all. Everything has been paid! Now there is nothing left for us to do but enjoy the fact that He calls us into an intimate relationship with Himself, made possible by a covenant paid for by His own blood.

No longer do we live in performance mode, trying to get God to be pleased with us and accept us. So many people waste prayer, frothing in guilt and unworthiness or trying to earn brownie points with God instead of simply believing the good news of the Gospel. But since He paid it all, there is nothing for us to do . . . except respond to His voice.

We need to be drenched with this understanding. We are His sons and daughters, and He wants to talk to us. We must refuse every stronghold of unworthiness and the lack of confidence, and we must come to Him boldly.

God Wants Intimacy with Us

Sometimes when we pray, we try to give God information He already knows. Meanwhile, He is trying to give us information that we do not know. Do you have a friend who does all the talking when you get together? Most of us have encountered these types, but it is far preferable when communication is a two-way street. Prayer is not just talking to God; it is making yourself available to let Him talk to you.

Remember that God has called us into a covenant—a relationship. It is no longer about our performance; it is a covenant of listening. It involves our response and obedience to Him.

It is easy to catch ourselves trying to perform and thinking, *I just need to read the Bible more and pray more. I just need to talk to people about the Lord more.* Those are all good things to do, but they are unnecessary to win God's acceptance and approval. We have already been approved and accepted by what He has accomplished, "to the praise of the glory of His grace, by which He made us accepted in the Beloved" (Ephesians 1:6).

My good friend Larry, who is a pastor, told me that upon waking up one morning, he heard the voice of the Lord say, "Intimacy can only occur when there is no fear of judgment."

Some think that God is going to scold us, judge us or rebuke us. The truth is that Jesus has taken our sins away and is not mad at us, and that the Holy Spirit is showing us how to walk with Him and listen to Him. Yes, He will correct us, but He does it in love, as does any good parent.

God desires intimacy with us, but if we see God as ready to judge us, we will run from Him. Guilt makes people run from God. The good news of the Gospel is that God is not only not mad at us—He has also taken every debt and the penalty of our sin upon Himself. Many Christians can quote John 3:16, "For God so loved the world that He gave His only begotten Son, that whoever believes in Him should not perish but have everlasting life." But when we talk about God's love, we need to include the verse that follows it: "For God did not send His Son into the world to condemn the world, but that the world through Him might be saved" (verse 17).

A New Level

God is not mad at anyone. He desires to reconcile every person to Himself. He has already provided the payment for our sins. He has made a way through the cross not only for our sins to be forgiven, but for us to enjoy intimacy with Him. In fact, we talk about learning to trust God, but He wants to take us to a point where He can trust us with more. He wants to take us to a new level. Jesus took His disciples to a new level:

> You are My friends if you do whatever I command you. No longer do I call you servants, for a servant does not know what his master is doing; but I have called you friends, for all things that I heard from My Father I have made known to you.
>
> John 15:14–15

Yes, God wants to talk to us. James is emphatic about this:

> If any of you lacks wisdom, let him ask of God, who gives to all liberally and without reproach, and it will be given to him. But let him ask in faith, with no doubting, for he who doubts

109

is like a wave of the sea driven and tossed by the wind. For let not that man suppose that he will receive anything from the Lord; he is a double-minded man, unstable in all his ways.

James 1:5–8

Double-mindedness means having two minds. One mind says, *I believe*, and another mind says, *I'm not worthy and I'm not sure.* We have to be convinced that God wants to give us an answer. If we are not convinced, why ask? God has promised to give us answers—liberally. He will not upbraid or scold us, telling us we are asking a stupid question. He wants us to come to His throne boldly, single-mindedly convinced that He will answer us.

Come Ready to Buy

One of the greatest truths the Lord has ever taught me is that when we come to Him, we must desire to receive something we previously did not have. We must realize that we will not leave His presence the same as when we came. In effect, we have to come before God with a willingness to buy. Isaiah 55:1 says, "Ho! Everyone who thirsts, come to the waters; and you who have no money, come, buy and eat. Yes, come, buy wine and milk without money and without price."

When we come before God in our individual prayer time or when we come as a part of a group of worshipers, the Holy Spirit wants us to maintain one passion—to buy from Him!

In many stores, a clerk will approach you and ask the classic question, "May I help you?"

We usually give the classic response, "No, thank you. I'm just looking."

I believe this also happens when we come to church or

110

spend time in prayer. The Holy Spirit asks us, "May I help you?"

If we live without expectation, we might answer, "No, thank You. I'm just being religious."

We must approach the Lord with a desire to buy something. In other words, I want to "buy" direction, healing, breakthrough, understanding and all the other things He offers. Sadly, most people do not buy from Him. Rather, they go through their religious motions, leaving church or their prayer time having "purchased" nothing.

When the woman with the issue of blood touched Jesus' clothes, He heard the cash register ring. His statement was, "Who touched Me? . . . I perceived power going out from Me" (Luke 8:45–46).

This woman was different from the crowds who were near Him. Because of her desperation and desire, she made a purchase from Him. She had to press through an entire crowd to make her purchase, just as we also have to press through a crowd of obstacles if we want to touch Him. The crowd we have to deal with is made up of distractions, discouragement, overwhelmedness, weariness, unbelief, fear, woundedness, unworthiness, fear of rejection and the like. But just like this woman, if we break through the crowd, we will get our breakthrough.

We have to ask ourselves, though, *Am I touching God, or am I waiting for Him to touch me?* I think it is hilarious that everyone in the crowd that day denied touching Jesus. In today's culture, we seem to do the same. "Yes, I've been at church hundreds of times, but I've never touched You." Many of us have the mentality of waiting for God to touch us, when all the while the opportunity awaits us to touch Him.

We are supposed to touch Him. Mark 6:56 is another Scripture that makes this clear: "Wherever He entered, into villages, cities, or the country, they laid the sick in the marketplaces, and begged Him that they might just touch the hem of His garment. And as many as touched Him were made well."

Notice that the verse says "as many as touched Him," not "as many as He touched." The bottom line is that the question is not whether God is going to touch you, but whether you are going to touch Him. How can you touch Him? By pressing into His presence with persistency and with a heart of expectation.

The Holy Spirit is 24/7

When people acknowledge that they believe in God, they have not exactly reached the heights of spiritual maturity. The devil does not fear what you and I believe, since he believes it himself. As James 2:19 says, "You believe that there is one God. You do well. Even the demons believe—and tremble!"

In fact, have you ever heard God referred to as "the Man upstairs" or "the good Lord"? Or have you ever had a person tell you, "Someone must be watching out for me?" Let me reemphasize that the devil is not afraid of such impersonal beliefs people have in God. He only fears your relationship with God. What the devil fears is the anointing—the active working power of the Holy Spirit in your life.

Christianity is far more than a set of beliefs—it is knowing who you are. It is a personal covenant with God through Jesus Christ. And this covenant promises fellowship and communication with the Holy Spirit, the orchestrator of the New Covenant. Hearing the Holy Spirit is the greatest experience known to man. Yet how many people live oblivious to the awesome knowledge that they can actively engage in conversation and communication with Him 24/7? The Holy Spirit is 24/7. He does not sleep. He is always available to give us wisdom and counsel concerning any situation.

The highest priority for all Christians, and especially for those in ministry, is to pay the price to take time to listen to God. There is no substitute for being in tune with the Holy Spirit. It does not matter how successful you perceive yourself to be. Your talent, great though it may be, is a poor substitute for hearing and heeding a fresh word from God. The flow of life from God's throne cannot be imitated. You need to come boldly to His throne.

Now that we have seen how important it is for us to come boldly to God's throne, in the next chapter let's examine the extreme significance of coming with expectation.

11

Live with Expectation

Expectation releases God's Kingdom into our situation. . . .

> In the morning, O LORD, you hear my voice;
> in the morning I lay my requests before you
> and wait in expectation.
>
> Psalm 5:3 NIV1984

It was a summer evening in July, and after a wonderful time with believers in a small-town church, I became aware that the Holy Spirit was not releasing me to close the meeting. I had a strong sense that He wanted to do something additional before I dismissed the people. It was frustrating because it seemed like a courtesy to say a closing prayer and send everyone on their way. Not knowing what to do, I struggled to listen. Then suddenly, the Holy Spirit gave me the strong impression to ask for someone who had served sixteen years in the military to identify himself or herself.

A lady seated on the back row raised her hand and softly stated, "My husband and I were in the military in Germany for sixteen years."

Relieved at this response, it seemed the obvious thing to do was to pray for her. As I prayed, still holding the microphone, words seemed just to flow out of my spirit. I was aware that the Lord was speaking comforting words through me, describing the ordeal she had been through and promising He would restore her.

The couple next to this lady were crying as I spoke out that comfort from the Lord. After the meeting, I was told that they had driven two hours to bring their friend. They had arrived with intense expectation, believing for a release of God's Kingdom power, praying and declaring, "Lord, we're not leaving this meeting until our friend gets some answers and comfort."

Her friends told me her story. A few months earlier, her daughter had been preparing to travel to Europe as a foreign-exchange student and was flying overseas the following day. The family stayed up until two o'clock in the morning to help her pack, until finally everyone went to bed exhausted. A lit candle was accidentally left burning, however, and its flame caught a curtain on fire, burning the entire house down. This woman's two daughters had died in the fire. She had come to the meeting that summer night in desperate need, and because her friends came with a strong expectation toward God, He ministered to her.

Hearing from God is dependent on our expectation toward Him. Expectation invites the power of the Holy Spirit to flow, just like an appliance's plugged-in cord pulls current out of an electrical outlet. God has plenty of power, but we have to "plug into Him" with expectation. This young couple understood the need for expectation and boldness. They were determined not to leave without hearing from Him.

Contrary to religious thinking and our own contrived unworthiness, God's presence faithfully abides in us. He does not come and go. Expectation pulls from Him. "But the anointing which you have received from Him *abides in you*" (1 John 2:27, emphasis added).

God is as close as our own breath. We only need to ask! He is willing to speak to us on any subject. He is speaking all the time. Television stations broadcast continually, but if you have no receiver, you will see and hear nothing. The airwaves continually enable millions of people at the same time to talk and text on cell phones. We cannot see the airwaves, but we can greatly enjoy their benefits. Christians need to develop their receivers—their human spirit—that enable them to tune in to the voice of the Holy Spirit. There is no question that He is available to speak to us anytime.

Two Expectation Killers

Learning about living with expectation has drastically altered my life. It is the key that opens the door to the miraculous. There are a couple things, though, that can kill our expectation.

The number one expectation killer is unworthiness. Feeling unworthy is a struggle we all face, but it is a stronghold we must deal with. The truth is, we have been made worthy. We have to believe the Gospel, shake off any sense of unworthiness and come boldly before His throne, as we talked about in the previous chapter.

Think about the stronghold of unworthiness that had Peter bound. Jesus performed such an over-the-top, mind-boggling miracle in directing them about where to cast their nets and catch some fish that you would think it would have triggered Peter's faith. Yet look at his response:

> And when they had done this, they caught a great number of fish, and their net was breaking. So they signaled to their partners in the other boat to come and help them. And they came and filled both the boats, so that they began to sink. When Simon Peter saw it, he fell down at Jesus' knees, saying, "Depart from me, for I am a sinful man, O Lord!"
>
> Luke 5:6–8

What a miracle! But Peter's response was "Depart from me, for I am a sinful man."

Jesus did not address Peter's self-imposed unworthiness; He simply declared, "Do not be afraid. From now on you will catch men" (verse 10).

Our unworthiness says, "Holy Spirit, get away from me." God wants us to focus on catching souls instead.

The second expectation killer is the religious statement, "If it be Thy will." Yes, Jesus prayed it. Luke's record tells us that in the garden, Jesus asked three times if there were another way to pay for humankind's sins. Then He surrendered, saying, "Father, if it is Your will, take this cup away from Me; nevertheless not My will, but Yours, be done" (Luke 22:42). This statement has been so taken out of context. Religion has twisted it in such a way that now it puts a disclaimer on all such prayers. It makes it seem as though we cannot exercise our faith for any request, because we always default to "If it be Thy will."

Yet God is willing to give us wisdom in any situation, and He tells us to ask and receive, that our joy may be full (see James 1:5;

John 16:24). What is His will? His will is abundant life, health, strength, victory and freedom. "For all the promises of God in Him are Yes, and in Him Amen, to the glory of God through us" (2 Corinthians 1:20). What does God require? He requires one thing—that we walk in the Spirit. Since Jesus paid it all, we must realize that all requirements are fulfilled one way—by not walking according to the flesh, but according to the Spirit:

> There is therefore now no condemnation to those who are in Christ Jesus, who do not walk according to the flesh, but according to the Spirit . . . that the righteous requirement of the law might be fulfilled in us who do not walk according to the flesh but according to the Spirit.
>
> Romans 8:1, 4

Is it that easy? Yes! When we stop trying to perform and stop dragging ourselves through guilt and condemnation, the fun begins. We simply need to believe the Gospel.

Along with two killers, expectation also has two enemies. They are *self-satisfaction* and *distractions*. Self-satisfaction alerts God that we do not want another drop. It declares a "don't call me, I'll call you" attitude. God will not invade the small world of the self-satisfied. In fact, He cannot, any more than a waiter can put more water into a full glass. God cannot give more to someone who is full and satisfied.

Distractions are traitors that keep us in bondage to the unimportant. Distracted saints live with no expectation toward God, because their time is occupied with lesser things.

Keeping a Record

To begin living a life of expectancy, it is extremely important to keep a record of everything God speaks to you. (Even note the dates when He speaks.) There is something about journaling what He speaks to us that invites Him to speak even more. No matter how simple what you hear seems—an unusual thought, something you might have heard in the night, a dream that has stuck with you, a picture, an impression you received, a sentence or a phrase that seemed to cross your spirit—*all* are worth recording.

Why keep a record? First of all, it is an act of expectation. This puts a pull or draw on the Holy Spirit. You are expecting God to talk to you. That posture of expectation puts you in a place of receptivity and assurance that you will hear Him. He wants you to hear His voice.

Second, you will be amazed at how quickly you can forget the thoughts you hear from God. For example, in the middle of the night you may awaken with a phrase or thought prominent in your spirit. You know you should get up and write it down, but your reasoning mind (and your sleepy body) agree that you will remember it in the morning.

Guess what—morning comes and you remember that you were going to write the thought down, but you do not remember what the thought was. Why? Anything that God speaks to you is *not a product of your reasoning mind or thought processes*. Whatever way His voice comes, it will bypass your intellectual reasoning process. It is given to your spirit. So when God speaks something once, we must diligently record it. My experience is that you will not get the Lord to repeat something to you the next day. In wisdom and good stewardship, we must keep a record so that we can refer back to what God has spoken.

There have been times when I have heard the Lord clearly and have written it down. Yet maybe a month later, I might read back through my notebook and realize that I have no recollection of some of the things I wrote, even though they are in my handwriting. Obviously, my spirit received the word, but my brain did not remember because it did not come from my brain.

Conversely, we can test what we "think" we have heard from God by observing how the thought came. Was it "dropped in" by the Holy Spirit or only part of the reasoning process our minds were going through at that moment? When the Lord "drops" knowledge into someone's spirit, it usually has nothing to do with the rationalizing process the mind is going through at the time. In fact, His voice (if we look back) actually interrupts our thought process.

For example, because you see something that reminds you of someone, a person whom you have not thought of for a long time may suddenly be on your mind. When the Lord speaks, however, the thought seems to come out of nowhere. It has nothing to do with our thought process. His voice is just there.

Tune in Early

How exciting it is that in the first few waking moments of every day, while our mind is still fresh, uncluttered and rousing out of sleep, the Holy Spirit will talk to us. It is as though He catches our brain off guard, and in those first few seconds and minutes, if we pay attention we will hear the Lord.

Use this time of awakening to set your spiritual tempo for the day. Take time to tune in early and listen to the Lord. You will hear strategies for the day for yourself, your family and the needs of the Kingdom. God will speak at any time of day, but it helps to become accustomed to hearing Him by tuning in early in the morning. If we start our day by thinking of all

120

that needs to be done, we have a tendency to shut God out of our thoughts. If we focus on Him, He will talk to us and direct our day. As Isaiah 50:4 says, "He awakens Me morning by morning, He awakens My ear to hear as the learned."

I have had the same experience upon drifting off to sleep. As my mind begins to relax, I often hear the Lord speak something. Even though my mind is groggy, my spirit is alert.

Of course, as we grow in the area of hearing the Lord, we can learn to discipline our mind to "step aside" when we need to hear the Lord concerning something. The brain is a wonderful gift from God, but it was created to be a servant, not a master. It becomes more and more obvious as we walk with God that the analytical mind can be the very thing that obstructs the flow of the Spirit and the voice of the Lord coming to us.

God is the ultimate intellect, and He is not against us using our reasoning minds. When it comes to the discipline of listening to the Holy Spirit, though, the mind can be distracted by "noise pollution," which frustrates our hearing from God. It can be as if two people are trying to carry on a quiet conversation while someone next to them is banging on a piano.

The good news is that the conscious mind sleeps, just like the rest of the body. Our mind shuts off when our body goes into slumber. Perhaps that is why some people hear from God in dreams. God has less trouble getting through to them when they are sleeping.

Never go to bed without a notebook and a pen on your nightstand, because you never know when God will speak to you. Then you can easily reach over and record anything you hear. Actually, be prepared at all times to write something down when God speaks. Doing this is an act of expectation and faith toward God. Ask Him to talk to you. We have already seen that He will speak, in so many ways.

Expectation—The Key to Hearing God

Let me say it again: Do not just pray . . . pray with expectation. In other words, be fully persuaded and anticipating that as you pray, you will hear and receive an answer. And remember that the way you hear God's voice may come in many forms, as we talked about in the first nine chapters.

Expectation is the key that unlocks the storehouses of heaven and opens the way for God to speak to us. Never pray without expectation. Expectation lets God know you are waiting for a response. He will always be faithful to answer an expectant heart. David said, "My soul, wait silently for God alone, for my expectation is from Him" (Psalm 62:5).

Expectation is also the key to the move of the Holy Spirit among the saints. When saints gather with anticipation, the Holy Spirit moves in response, no matter who ministers in front of the people.

Do you want to hear from God? Live with expectation. Pray with expectation. Listen with expectation. You *will* hear His voice.

Now that we have talked about coming boldly to His throne and living with expectation, in the next chapter let's recognize the need for keeping it simple. Life is complicated enough without complicating the simplicity of the Gospel, which is meant to be the Good News that everyone can understand.

12

Keep It Simple

Do not complicate the Gospel.

Few people could go into their garage and build an automobile. The task would be far too complex. In fact, the majority of people have little idea how a car functions. Although numerous physical and engineering laws are involved in the fabrication of a car, the manufacturer has reduced driving a car to simplicity for the purpose of the consumer. Most adults can drive a car, and for one reason—the manufacturer has taken a complicated feat of engineering and reduced it to turning a key in the ignition and using the steering wheel, gear shift, accelerator and brakes.

Many inventions take a complicated task or piece of equipment and reduce it to simplicity. Likewise, God has taken the complicated issues of the world and reduced the answers to all life's questions into the simplicity of the Gospel. For example, this is simple: One died for all. "For He made Him who knew no sin to be sin for us, that we might become the righteousness of God in Him" (2 Corinthians 5:21).

In fact, one way we can be convinced we have heard from God is that the answer is simple. Jesus took complicated problems of blindness, leprosy and paralysis and simplified them into obedience. "Go wash." "Go show yourselves to the priest." "Take up your bed and walk."

Hearing God's voice does not mean we understand all the mysteries of the world. It means God will articulate a word or command that will simplify, heal and deliver us in *our* situation.

Paul the apostle was a powerful man of God who seemed to fear nothing. He had been through beatings, shipwrecks and all kinds of persecution. Yet he did express one fear: "But I fear, lest somehow, as the serpent deceived Eve by his craftiness, so your minds may be corrupted from the simplicity that is in Christ" (2 Corinthians 11:3).

Think about it. The only fear Paul had was that we would miss the simplicity of the Gospel. I do not think there is any question that the Gospel of Christ gets overcomplicated. In fact, God promises to make it so simple that even a fool will not miss it. Talking about the Highway of Holiness, Isaiah 35:8 tells us, "Whoever walks the road, although a fool, shall not go astray."

Paul also acted with extreme compassion. Instead of trying to wow everyone with his intellect, he laid it down so that the faith of those who listened to him would not rest in man's wisdom, but in God's power. That was a true act of selflessness:

And I, brethren, when I came to you, did not come with excellence of speech or of wisdom declaring to you the testimony of God. For I determined not to know anything among you except Jesus Christ and Him crucified. I was with you in weakness, in fear, and in much trembling. And my speech and my preaching were not with persuasive words of human wisdom, but in demonstration of the Spirit and of power, that your faith should not be in the wisdom of men but in the power of God.

1 Corinthians 2:1–5

Innocence and Humility

Before Adam and Eve sinned, they lived in a state of innocence. There was no such thing as good and evil. But as soon as their eyes were opened, they lost their innocence (see Genesis 3:7). One problem we have in the Body of Christ is that although we have been saved and redeemed, we have not regained our innocence. Although new creations, we are still eating from the tree of the knowledge of good and evil, not from the Tree of Life.

Eating from the tree of the knowledge of good and evil means we have become judges and look at things through our own perspective, not God's. But Jesus insisted that we come to Him as little children. When it comes to listening to the Holy Spirit, we must approach Him with childlike innocence. He told us in Matthew 18:3–5,

Assuredly, I say to you, unless you are converted and become as little children, you will by no means enter the kingdom of heaven. Therefore whoever humbles himself as this little child is the greatest in the kingdom of heaven. Whoever receives one little child like this in My name receives Me.

Jesus rejoiced over this principle that God actually hides things from the "worldly wise." Look at His words in Luke 10:21:

In that hour Jesus rejoiced in the Spirit and said, "I praise You, Father, Lord of heaven and earth, that You have hidden these things from the wise and prudent and revealed them to babes. Even so, Father, for so it seemed good in Your sight."

God "resists the proud, but gives grace to the humble" (1 Peter 5:5). He wants us to come to Him with trusting, childlike and nonanalytical obedience. God has not only "made foolish the wisdom of this world" (1 Corinthians 1:20), but He also uses the foolish things of the world for His purposes:

But God has chosen the foolish things of the world to put to shame the wise, and God has chosen the weak things of the world to put to shame the things which are mighty; and the base things of the world and the things which are despised God has chosen, and the things which are not, to bring to nothing the things that are.

1 Corinthians 1:27–28

A friend of mine made a statement years ago that has always stuck with me: "The devil can't do much with humility."

What a simple but profound truth. The devil has no strategy to deal with true humility. The Holy Spirit, like water, flows at the lowest level. Water will not flow uphill. The Holy Spirit will not flow up mountains of arrogance and pride, but only flows in the valleys of humility.

Humility has a lot to do with innocence. "Behold, I send you out as sheep in the midst of wolves," Jesus said. "Therefore be wise as serpents and harmless [innocent] as doves" (Matthew 10:16).

When I was a young pastor, I had been preaching a great deal on the subject of salvation, and I emphasized continually that no one "earns" his way with God. One night after preaching on this for several weeks, I awoke from sleep and the Holy Spirit spoke one inaudible but distinct sentence to me.

He said, "No, you don't earn your way; you *obey* your way."

That simple sentence has helped me so much through the years. Growth in God comes by obedience . . . perpetual obedience.

Another time, for hours I had been preparing a teaching on idolatry. Then a few minutes before I stood up to preach, I prayed silently, "Lord, what is idolatry?"

Immediately He answered me, "Whatever is foremost on your mind."

That simple word from the Holy Spirit cut through all the complexities of the subject and gave me an answer in one sentence that has stayed with me all my life. Thank God for intelligent and gifted minds, but the things of the Spirit bypass the natural mind and are revealed by the Spirit.

Simplicity does not imply simple-mindedness, of course. Simplicity could better be defined as having the key. What good is a beautiful house or a nice car without a key? When God gives us the key to something (through revelation), the awesome becomes attainable and uncomplicated.

For example, the key to the miraculous is expectation. The key to love is forgiveness. The key to the heart of God is worship. The key to deliverance is repentance. The key to faith is obedience.

As you endeavor to hear the voice of the Lord, pay attention to the Holy Spirit inside you. He has the key to unlock any situation. One word from God dispels all obscurity and confusion. This is ultimate Christianity—communication and communion with the Holy Spirit, along with knowing more and more about Jesus, the author and finisher of our faith.

Revealed, Not Figured Out

Analytical minds do not get far trying to understand the dimensions of the Spirit. No wonder the apostle Paul prayed "that the God of our Lord Jesus Christ, the Father of glory, may give to you the spirit of wisdom and revelation in the knowledge of Him, the eyes of your understanding being enlightened" (Ephesians 1:17–18).

God is revealed, *not figured out.* That is why hearing the voice of God is so exciting. When the Holy Spirit conveys truth, the revelation is so simple, yet so profound in its ramifications. But again, we have to come to Him as innocent children. One thing people admire about children is their innocence. We are told to be the same way. God hides things from the intellectually proud. He requires childlike faith and humility:

> Then Jesus called a little child to Him, set him in the midst of them, and said, "Assuredly, I say to you, unless you are converted and become as little children, you will by no means enter the kingdom of heaven. Therefore whoever humbles himself as this little child is the greatest in the kingdom of heaven. Whoever receives one little child like this in My name receives Me."
>
> Matthew 18:2–5

People often ask me how they can hear from God. The first thing I emphasize is that *how* is not as important as *where.* I have already said that God does not talk to our brain. He speaks to our spirit. Jesus never said that living water would flow out of your *head.* He said out of your *heart* will flow rivers of living water (see John 7:38). The Holy Spirit *within* the believer will communicate truth.

Look at Proverbs 3:5–6: "Trust in the LORD with all your heart, and lean not on your own understanding; in all your

ways acknowledge Him, and He shall direct your paths."
Notice it does not say, "Trust in the Lord with all your brain."
It says "with all your heart."

Many believers go through their entire lives little recognizing the power of God, because they are assuming that anything God does will be sensational and spectacular. Usually
the opposite is true. God may not typically speak or move in
ways that are sensational, but He is there. Along with coming boldly to His throne, living with expectation and keeping it simple, we also need to avoid the sensational and the
spectacular. Let's talk more about that in the next chapter.

13

Look beyond the Spectacular

If you look for the spectacular, you will miss the supernatural. . . .

> But the LORD was not in the wind; and after the wind an earthquake, but the LORD was not in the earthquake; and after the earthquake a fire, but the LORD was not in the fire; and after the fire *a still small voice.*
>
> 1 Kings 19:11–12, emphasis added

The greatest hindrance to the supernatural is the spectacular. The spectacular stands in the way of recognizing the supernatural power of God. It is our human nature to want to stereotype God into a sensational paradigm. We reason that since God is big, then whatever He says or does will be big or dramatic. But the opposite is true. The bigness comes

130

in our faith to trust His still, small voice. Who could not pay attention to an audible voice? But it does take faith to pay attention to the still, small inner voice and witness of the Holy Spirit. We cannot please God without faith (see Hebrews 11:6).

Many Christians express frustration that they cannot hear the voice of the Lord, but it is because they are still waiting for a spectacular sound. Leaders have trained people to respond to sensation instead of to the voice of God, but the primary requirement for hearing from God is merely the willingness to listen to the still, small voice.

Hearing God's voice should not be a rare or once-in-a-lifetime occurrence, and His voice most likely will not be audible (although a few claim to have heard Him audibly). To hear God only when His voice is audible would almost be a sure indication that He dwells *outside* your temple, not *inside*. He lives inside your temple, however, not outside.

Ultimately, the Lord desires that we *live a life of listening*. It takes discipline to command all manner of distractions to be still while we wait before God. Yet how can anyone have a successful ministry in God's eyes without hearing and communing with the Holy Spirit on a continual basis?

Four Don'ts

Years ago, the Lord illuminated these four truths to me:

1. *Don't accept Christ . . . follow Him.* We have wrongly taught people to "accept" Christ (which is not in the Bible), so people accept Him but never *follow* Him. Jesus was not looking for acceptance, but for followers.
2. *Don't read the Bible . . . study it.* Paul did not write, "Read to show yourself approved." He wrote, "Study

to shew thyself approved unto God, a workman that needeth not to be ashamed, rightly dividing the word of truth" (2 Timothy 2:15 KJV). You will not get much out of the Bible simply by reading it; you have to study it. Just as you cannot simply read a chemistry book; you have to study it.

3. *Don't pray . . . listen.* Prayer often can be just an articulation of your anguish and frustration, or it can be saying things you think God wants to hear. But prayer is more listening and responding.

4. *Don't go to church . . . be the Church.* We are not supposed to just go to church; we are supposed to be the Church. When we see ourselves "going to church," we forget that every day we are the Body of Christ, carrying the Holy Spirit to a hurting world. The best way to put it is this: We are the Church going to a meeting.

Keys to Hearing the Lord

Over the years, it has become evident to me that whether I am praying about a major decision or a very simple issue, the voice of the Lord is not one bit louder either way. At one time this frustrated me, because logic says God would speak more dramatically concerning big decisions and show less enthusiasm about small decisions. But He does not. Why? Because the Holy Spirit does not change. He still requires that in faith, we *respond* and *act* on the still, small voice we hear. Let's look at several keys I have discovered in regard to hearing the Lord.

1. Do not demand that His voice be sensational. It rarely will be.

2. Reject the fear of failure. You are free to fail. But you are not free to be irresponsible. Admit it when you thought

132

you heard God, but the outcome proves you did not. I like to use the term *trial and error*, because learning to hear God is a process, and we have to be willing to miss it sometimes.

3. Stay stirred up. Do not let your inner man get into a dormant state, as it will when it has been several days since you prayed with intensity. Prayer and praise stir up your receptivity to the still, small voice of God. Stay in an attitude of anticipation and expectation.

4. Because the spoken word is creative, realize that the devil hates the fact that you hear from God. Resist him when he opposes your taking time to pray and listen to God (see James 4:7). I believe this is so key for us to remember. The devil uses distractions, disruptive thoughts, worry and all sorts of "weapons" to hinder our posture in listening to God.

5. Recognize that the mind is the greatest obstacle to hearing. You must command your mind to shift into neutral and not hold onto strife or strong opinions. Then exercise your spirit with thanksgiving, praise and prayer until you sense God's presence and peace.

6. It is essential to pray in the Spirit. Your prayer language opens the human spirit to hear the Lord. "But you, beloved, building yourselves up on your most holy faith, praying in the Holy Spirit, keep yourselves in the love of God" (Jude 1:20–21).

Expect and Anticipate

Expect God to speak. Not someday, but today. Listen as you are praying. Many do not hear from God because they live with no expectation about His willingness to speak. You must have no uncertainty about His willingness. You will not *expect* to hear God if you feel condemnation (that harsh, judgmental feeling, or guilt because you feel you do not measure up) that the devil tries to convince you is from God. You must rebuke the enemy, shake off those feelings and approach the Lord as an innocent child, expecting Him to speak.

As you approach God for any type of direction, whether large or small, *first* recognize that you are coming to the Lord who is *willing* to give you the answer in a liberal, generous, noncondemning way. Encourage yourself with that fact. You are approaching a giving God who wants to speak to you. James 1:5 tells us, "If any of you lacks wisdom, let him ask of God, who gives to all liberally and without reproach, and it will be given to him."

Another important point is to pray about one thing at a time. Although most of us mean well, many times we pray in generalities. In one prayer, we might pray for certain missionaries, the government and a neighbor, and then throw in a few questions about our job, our children and our need for direction. I have learned that it is much more productive to pray in specifics. This is vitally important. When you seek God for an answer, for wisdom or for direction, ask one question at a time. I emphasize this because if you are praying about more than one thing and the Holy Spirit shows you something, you will be confused about which prayer subject the picture, phrase or Scripture He gives you is referring to.

When you pray and ask God a specific question, you must believe that in the next few moments, He will speak to you. Trust what you hear or see, and what you sense He is saying to you. Your confidence will grow as He helps you discern and recognize His voice, no matter how faintly it comes. As you pray about each subject, record what the Lord shows you. The key is that His voice will not be sensational, and may, in fact, be very faint. But what He is showing you is precisely what you are praying about. You will gain confidence the more you are willing to trust the smallest impressions.

One of my greatest struggles in hearing God, whether I am alone or speaking in front of a group, is that because His voice is so quiet, I find myself questioning if I am making up the answers I am hearing. Through experience, however, I have found that although His voice may be faint, it is extremely accurate.

When you pray about a situation, it is good to ask the Lord how to pray. For example, if someone in your life refuses to have anything to do with the things of God, the Lord may show you how to pray for that person. He may want you to pray that He will create a spiritual hunger in that person, or to pray that He will send influential believers across his or her path. Or He may want you to bind and rebuke a spirit of spiritual blindness. Whatever God reveals to you to pray will bring results.

Deal with a Wandering Mind

In prayer we must guard against our minds wandering. We are all guilty of this, and I believe most people struggle in this area. We must focus and concentrate on the Lord in order to pinpoint what the voice of the Spirit is communicating to us.

When my mind begins to wander, I have found it helpful to write down the interruptions that come to mind. It seems as though the enemy (who hates our prayer and communication with God) will "remind" me of tasks at hand as soon as I begin to pray. Calmly, I write down the "to-dos" to save for later, and then I continue to focus on the specifics I am praying about.

The good news of the Gospel is that God is speaking all the time. He does not speak intermittently; we just hear intermittently. Once again, we have to recognize that our own active mind is our worst enemy. The "noisy" and wandering mind obstructs the voice of the Holy Spirit. We are geared to the natural and earthly realm, which constantly provides visual or sensual stimuli that provoke a response in us. This "busyness" has become ingrained in us to such a point that sitting quietly before the Lord seems foreign, so we declare it boring and fruitless. Obviously, we have not trained our spirit to listen. But with His help, we can subject our active and anxious mind to His presence.

That is precisely the reason that the crux of prayer is praying until we step into a realm of peace. It is somewhat like leaving a room where a party is going on and walking into a room of total silence. In prayer, as we persevere, we leave that loud "room" with all the cares of the day and enter into the "room" where we are more conscious of the quiet yet awesome and potent presence of the Lord. It is in this peaceful and quiet place that our mind becomes subject to the presence of the Lord. Then we can begin to hear what He is declaring from His throne.

Exercise Your Spiritual Man

I have a close friend, John, who is the pastor of a great church. We frequently talk by phone and have learned to pray together. It is not unusual for him to call me with a prayer request.

Hearing his need when he calls, I will say, "I promise to pray about that."

John will answer, "No, pray right now and see what the Holy Spirit tells you."

So I stop and pray, believing with him for wisdom from the Lord.

Seconds later, when I tell him what I am hearing or seeing, usually John will say, "That's exactly what I felt the Lord was saying to me."

The Holy Spirit is willing to give us wisdom right on the spot. But the same way the physical body needs exercise, our spiritual man needs exercise. Exercise listening to God. Pray about things, and then listen.

Sometimes it is good exercise to pray with your spouse or a good friend. Pray together and then ask one another, "What did you sense when we prayed?" Compare what you experienced. Did you see a picture or hear a phrase, a word or a Scripture?

Paul told us this about when the Body assembles: "How is it then, brethren? Whenever you come together, each of you has a psalm, has a teaching, has a tongue, has a revelation, has an interpretation. Let all things be done for edification" (1 Corinthians 14:26).

It is good to take every opportunity to exercise hearing from the Lord. I exercise my spiritual man all the time. Often, I ask the Holy Spirit's input on a purchase, whether it is buying a shirt, a car or a home. He knows the end from the beginning and even knows our tastes and preferences.

A number of years ago, we were in the process of purchasing a house. I was battling with fear because the home we were considering was a little above our price range.

One night as I lay in bed, I asked, "Lord, confirm the purchase to me again."

I heard these words from Him in reply: "Surrounded by capital gain."

Months later, I saw the builder of the home I purchased.

He told me that it was good I bought the house when I did, because the price of the exact same house had risen considerably. The Holy Spirit does not lie.

I believe where we all fall short of the purpose of God is that we fail to *stay* in the realm of the Spirit. Paul stated, "In Him we live and move and have our being" (Acts 17:28). For us, being in the realm of the Spirit ought to be a perpetual state. He abides in us and we abide in Him (see John 15:4). Yet we have conditioned ourselves to coming back and forth into the presence of God, rather than living by the reality that we are *in* His presence perpetually.

When we envision ourselves as coming to and going from God's presence, we lose faith that He hears us, and we lack confidence in the fact that He is closer than our own breath. This coming-and-going mentality robs us dramatically, and makes hearing the Lord far more difficult than He intended. Yet Jesus told us, "For My yoke is easy and My burden is light" (Matthew 11:30). We waste a lot of time trying to get *back* into the presence of the Lord, trying to feel worthy and trying to believe that He has made us righteous, so we can somehow feel that it is all right to come boldly (see Hebrews 10:19).

One thing I have learned about the Holy Spirit is that He has a wonderful capacity (as He lives in you and me) to be accessed or stirred up. However, it is *up to us* to do so. Frankly, He waits, available but unrecognized in the heart of the majority of Christians. We can stir Him up through praise, prayer and gratitude. Paul exhorted Timothy to "stir up the gift of God which is in you" (2 Timothy 1:6).

The cell phone is a perfect example. No matter who your carrier is, they do not come to your house and charge your phone for you. However, they do sell you a charger with the phone. Your phone will look the same whether it is charged or not, but it does not take long to realize that if you do not keep the phone charged, it will stop working.

In the same way, God has given us the Holy Spirit, but we have to use our charger—our will—to access His presence. Praise and worship stir Him. A thankful heart stirs Him. Intense prayer (even for a few minutes) stirs Him. He is worth it. He is worth pursuing.

Reject the Fear of Failure

I mentioned earlier that we are free to fail, but not free to be irresponsible. If we miss it trying to hear God, we just need to admit it. One of the greatest freedoms God gives each of us is the freedom to fail. This concept is implied throughout the Scripture. We have freedom to make mistakes. In fact, when we try so hard not to miss hearing God, we can more easily miss Him because striving and straining will quench the Spirit.

A common bondage in many Christian circles is the undermining fear that says, "Whatever you do, don't miss the Lord!" I do not see the heart of God that way. We learn by trial and error—by recognizing mistakes and pitfalls by way of experience. Thomas Edison's philosophy regarding failures was that he had just found another way that did not work. He never let that stop him from continuing his experiments.

Life is a classroom. We are learning to know God and His ways. There is no condemnation as long as we endeavor to learn from and walk before Him. He teaches us and uses us at the same time. School never ends; there is always more to learn.

Embrace the freedom you have to make mistakes, and then pursue listening to God. If you thought you heard Him and circumstances prove later that you did not, just acknowledge it. The only thing at stake is your pride, and God insists that pride be crucified anyway. Remember James 4:6, "God resists the proud, but gives grace to the humble."

Our Greatest Priority

Demonic powers tremble at the prophetic realm. Our enemy knows that any time the Holy Spirit speaks to us, He speaks with creative power. No wonder our adversary strategizes ways to block and confuse us, and to get us distracted and preoccupied, which obstructs our ability to hear the words of the Holy Spirit.

Once God speaks to us and we embrace what He is saying, it is too late for our adversary to steal that word. Creative power is issuing forth. The more we live with this understanding, the more we realize that our greatest priority as Christians is to stay in tune with God. We must aggressively oppose any obstacle, distraction or discouragement that would prevent us from hearing Him.

Once again, we must keep in mind that as creative as His words are, they do not always come audibly in a spectacular, sensational voice. In fact, they rarely come that way. It is His still, small voice we are listening for most intently. In the next chapter, we will talk about how our confidence grows as we develop our ability to hear that voice by finding our spiritual equilibrium.

14

Find Your Spiritual Equilibrium

We must find our own center of gravity in our relationship with God.

Work out your own salvation with fear and
trembling.

Philippians 2:12

When children are learning to walk, they fall down many times.
Since they are close to the ground, there is rarely an injury. Plus,
their soft bones provide built-in protection from breakage. No
parent is upset with a child taking spills, because those simply
are part of the learning process. The child is discovering his
or her center of equilibrium. The more a new walker falls and
gets back up, the more the child becomes acquainted with his
or her own sense of balance and center of gravity.

Spiritually speaking, each of us must find our own center
of equilibrium in our ability to *hear* and *recognize* the voice

of the Holy Spirit. We can learn from others, but ultimately we must have our own experiences. In the previous chapters, we looked at specific ways we can hear from God. We have to exercise ourselves hearing in these ways until we are comfortable with our experiences.

In the first few years of my Christian experience, I was highly impressed by those who mentored me, and I envied the way they could hear from the Lord so accurately. But soon I began to have my own experiences. Through the years, I have learned to recognize a number of little ways that I know God is talking to me. These are personal to me—little nudges, the way He brings things back to my remembrance, certain feelings I get deep down in my spirit, the way He checks my spirit or prompts me. It is like the way a husband and wife learn to communicate and know one another. They share little things to laugh over, a certain look, a raised eyebrow—all things no one else would understand that develop out of their unique relationship.

Similarly, we learn to know and communicate with God. We develop a unique relationship and find our own center of gravity in our walk with Him. We all use many forms of communication besides talking. A nod, a wave, a smile, a thumbs-up, a facial expression . . . the list goes on. With experience, we understand God's different ways of speaking to us personally: His promptings, His nudges, His warning signals and so forth. We learn to know when we have a witness from Him and when He is showing us that we are going a wrong direction.

The bottom line is that we have to trust our inside (the center of our being), where the Holy Spirit dwells. If we do not learn to trust the Spirit within us, then we are living divorced from our inside and out of touch with His still, small voice. *Trust* is a key word because it is all about trusting what God is revealing to us in our inner man.

In our world, we face so many outside stimuli that can distract us. Even Christians are taught to look elsewhere for information rather than trusting the voice of the Lord within. But from the very beginning of our Christian walk, God speaks to us within our spirit, because that is where He lives. Although previously our spirit was dead unto God, we now have been made alive unto Him: "And you He made alive, who were dead in trespasses and sins" (Ephesians 2:1). Light has come to the spirits of humankind; therefore, it is in our spirit that God will guide and lead us. As Proverbs 20:27 says, "The spirit of a man is the lamp of the Lord." Our spirit man is pure and whole. It is our flesh that must be ruled by the Spirit.

Risky Earthen Vessels

God took a risk when He put the Holy Spirit in us—vessels who have all sorts of weaknesses and problems. Yet 2 Corinthians 4:7 says, "We have this treasure in earthen vessels, that the excellence of the power may be of God and not of us."

God does not have confidence in us, but in the Holy Spirit in us. When we understand that this glorious Gospel is not about us, but about the treasure of the Holy Spirit in us, we can enjoy freedom. Freedom from guilt and performance. Freedom to listen and obey. Notice that God did not say He put the treasure in perfect vessels or golden vessels or diamond vessels, but in earthen vessels. Why? "That the excellence of the power may be of God and not of us."

Outside stimuli, church activities and busyness in general seem to crowd out God's voice, which we were so thirsty to hear at the beginning of our walk with Him. Maybe that is why the writer of Hebrews said that some spiritual things were hard to explain "since you have become dull of hearing"

(Hebrews 5:11). God started us out with good ears, but they have grown dull when it comes to hearing Him.

It is our responsibility to cultivate our relationship with God so that we can hear Him. He commands us to seek Him and declares, "[I] will be found by you" (1 Chronicles 28:9). He promises that we will find Him when we seek Him with all our heart and soul (see Deuteronomy 4:29).

Cultivating the ability to know and hear God takes time, but He is the faithful Teacher if we will walk with openness before Him. In fact, He teaches us continually. Once we take on the posture of learning from Him, we begin to sense that He is showing us things on a 24-hour basis.

God uses everything He has created to teach us about Himself. We cannot look at the heavens without thinking of His vastness; we cannot look at the mountains without thinking of His majesty; we cannot look at a rushing river without thinking of the powerful flowing of the Holy Spirit; we cannot look at a fire without acknowledging His consuming presence. When we look at a tree, we should remember that when the seed of the Gospel has been sown in young believers, God's intention is to make them grow strong, tall and stable. Everything He has created describes the unseen world. In other words, God created the "seen" world in order to reveal to us the "unseen" world.

Work Out Your Own Salvation

Spiritual growth comes not only by hearing, but by doing. Believers grow by having their own experiences in the Holy Spirit. The only way to learn how to navigate on a computer is by actually doing it. No matter how thoroughly someone explains the process, you only become proficient by doing it yourself. So it is with spiritual growth:

Therefore, my beloved, as you have always obeyed, not as in my presence only, but now much more in my absence, work out your own salvation with fear and trembling; for it is God who works in you both to will and to do for His good pleasure.

Philippians 2:12–13

Why with fear and trembling? Because we could miss it. We could go through life undeveloped and remain in an immature, lifeless state. We have to endeavor to work at developing our relationship with God—just like working on a marriage relationship or exercising our physical body.

New believers are often paralyzed because their leaders make them dependent on the hearing skills of the leadership instead of teaching them to press into God themselves. A good leader's goal should be to teach other believers dependency on the Holy Spirit.

Confidence is paramount in hearing God. Most people struggle with the good news of the Gospel; they find it hard to believe that they can have an intimate relationship with God. Thus, it becomes a temptation to rely on the maturity of someone else whom they look up to—someone who gets his or her prayers answered more quickly. But God encourages us to have confidence, and He desires that *our* personal relationship with Him develop and mature.

Nothing stunts growth more than becoming too people dependent. A wise leader can discourage this by asking a person who wants prayer for direction, "What is the Lord telling you about this? What are you hearing?" Then it is good to pray with the person, and at the end of the prayer ask, "What did you sense the Holy Spirit saying about this when we prayed?" This approach demands that the person asking for prayer grow and recognize that he or she has the same Holy Spirit inside as the leader.

Trust What You Hear

Trusting what you hear is paramount. Many people hear the Holy Spirit, but do not trust what they hear. For example, if someone who is before the people is quenching the Holy Spirit, we may momentarily recognize it. But if we see that others are enthusiastic and accepting, we think, *Something must be wrong with me.* We lack confidence in the Spirit of God within us, although He is clearly speaking to us (see 1 John 2:27).

I went through this a few years ago, when everyone was enthused about a particular evangelist. A friend went with me to hear him twice, but we both felt grieved in our spirit. It was frustrating because of the excitement of the people around us. But it was not long before it proved true that he was full of improprieties. Many who endorsed him later were red-faced that they had not been more discerning.

When we endeavor to listen to the Holy Spirit ourselves, it soon becomes evident that we are in tune with Him. For example, when we hear an anointed sermon, we might realize, *That's the same thing I've been "hearing" all week.* Those kinds of experiences help us develop our spiritual equilibrium and help us become more and more steady on our feet, so to speak. If we ask the Holy Spirit, He will tell us things. And if our heavenly Father knows the number of hairs on billions of people's heads (see Luke 12:7), He certainly has time to listen and talk to us.

In the next chapter, let's talk more specifically about inquiring in God's temple. What an amazing thing it is that we are the temple where the Holy Spirit dwells, and that we can inquire of the One who lives within us.

15

Inquire in His Temple

It is fun to seek the Lord!

> One thing I have desired of the LORD, that
> will I seek: that I may dwell in the house of
> the LORD all the days of my life, to behold
> the beauty of the LORD, and to inquire in
> His temple.

> Psalm 27:4

David, being a man after God's own heart, loved the presence of God (see Acts 13:22). It inspires me to think of how
David loved to seek the Lord—"to inquire in His temple."
In the Old Testament, the people went to the Temple, which
had an outer court, an inner court and the holy of holies.
Now, *we* are the temple. We have a body (outer court), a soul
(inner court) and a spirit (holy of holies). "Or do you not

147

know that your body is the temple of the Holy Spirit who is in you, whom you have from God, and you are not your own?" (1 Corinthians 6:19).

Since we are the temple where the Holy Spirit dwells, we can inquire of the One who lives within us. We can hear from Him in our spirit, our holy of holies, in which He dwells. During my first years as a Spirit-filled Christian, I was privileged to spend time in the company of people who loved seeking the Lord. I remember being so hungry for the things of God that I could not wait for the times when a group of us would get together to sing and pray on a Friday night in someone's home. After a fervent time of worship, we would begin seeking the Lord about various things concerning the Kingdom of God, as well as inquiring about our personal lives.

It was amazing how clearly the Lord would speak to each of us. In fact, if five or six of us were praying and we all asked the Lord a specific question, we would usually come up with the identical answer from the Lord. One might hear a phrase, another might see a picture, another might receive a Scripture and so forth (see 1 Corinthians 14:26). Although the answer would come to each person in a different way, what each of us heard would wonderfully convey the same message.

I remember we had a prayer meeting one night when I was just eighteen and getting ready to go to college. After praying about some spiritual needs, my mentors shared how they were in the market for another car. They prayed about one car they had considered, and one person in the group saw a picture of a swaybacked horse. They concluded that the car would be a bad choice. As they prayed about another car, someone saw it as a cream puff. The next day, my mentor went to the used car lot and told the salesman he wanted that specific car.

"Do you want to take it for a test drive?" the salesman asked. "Don't you at least want to look under the hood?"

"No," my mentor replied. "I'll take it."

He signed the paperwork and drove it home. That car served them flawlessly for years.

I felt fortunate being among these people. It had never seemed possible to me that the Lord would actually speak to us. From praying with these seasoned Christians, I quickly learned how willing the Holy Spirit is to communicate with His people. I also quickly recognized that He communicates in many different ways.

Pray and Expect to Hear

During my first few weeks around these fervent people, one of the spiritually mature ladies commented, "The more you grow in God, the fainter His voice becomes."

That shocked me because I was struggling to hear the Spirit. Later, the Lord helped me understand that similar to a marriage relationship, I would begin to know Him better the longer I was with Him. You do not have to be reintroduced to your spouse every day—you know your spouse. You do not have to say, "Hey, do you remember me?" The two of you can communicate with a look and know each other's thoughts. In the same way, we begin to know God and recognize His voice as we become familiar with it.

Prayer is a two-way conversation. Whenever we pray, we should *expect* to hear something. What kind of conversation is it when only one person talks? God is not the least bit interested in our offering Him lip service. "This people honors Me with their lips, but their heart is far from Me" (Mark 7:6). He wants the channels of communication opened.

149

Do not just pray—listen. Then trust what you hear, faint though it may be.

It is good to inquire of the Lord. If something is bothering you, ask the Lord why. Then listen to what He says. He abides within you. He will show you. For example, at one point the Lord would not release me to accept invitations to minister. For a period of time, He wanted me to wait on Him. After a few months I grew impatient, so one day I asked Him how much longer until He would release me to travel and minister again. As I prayed, I received a picture in my spirit of a cook standing by a stove, slowing stirring what was cooking. Immediately, I understood what the Lord was saying. Release was near, but the waiting was not quite finished. The process needed a little more time. When He finally gave the release, it had been five months. The Scripture the Lord quickened to me was, "Then Jesus returned in the power of the Spirit to Galilee, and news of Him went out through all the surrounding region" (Luke 4:14). I experienced a fresh anointing and new power after that time of waiting.

Ask and You Shall Receive

We miss so much by not asking the Lord specific questions about things we are going through—why certain things have happened, what certain Scriptures mean and so forth.

One day, I asked the Lord about the lack of the move of the Spirit in the Church and why there is so much emphasis on personality and talent.

He said, "I'm looking for yielded vessels." Then He added, "Talent won't get the job done."

Talent alone, without anointing, accomplishes little.

He also said, "Natural abilities cannot bring forth the fruit of the Spirit."

On another occasion, I sought Him concerning why we encounter resistance so often from the devil.

He answered, "Resistance makes your spirit strong."

If God protected us from every type of resistance or conflict, we would never become spiritually strong. Just as exercise brings strength to the physical man, exercising the spirit brings strength to the spiritual man. Growth in God does not happen automatically; it requires that we exercise our spiritual muscles. And you cannot become strong by watching someone else exercise.

God wants us to inquire of Him. We are not putting Him to any trouble or irritating Him by asking for wisdom and understanding. He will answer generously: "If any of you is deficient in wisdom, let him ask of the giving God [Who gives] to every one liberally and ungrudgingly, without reproaching or faultfinding, and it will be given him" (James 1:5 AMPLIFIED).

The disciples asked the Lord the meaning of parables He had taught. "Explain to us the parable of the tares of the field," they said one time (Matthew 13:36).

The fact that the disciples asked was indicative not only of their hunger, but also of the fact that they did not feel intimidated by Him. He was approachable. The Holy Spirit is still approachable. He is more than willing to talk to us about anything we want to talk about. He definitely is not irritated by any question we wish to ask.

Listen and Learn

As I mentioned earlier, life is a classroom. Listening to God is a learning process, and it is unreasonable to believe that any and every thought that comes our way is automatically God speaking. However, we can learn to know and recognize His voice.

There are times when the Holy Spirit will simply "drop" things into our heart, nearly knocking us over, but those instances prove rare. In general, the Holy Spirit will talk to you and me specifically as we ask Him specifically.

One time, a television show contacted me about ministering on the program. The person representing the program told me of its far-reaching impact and how many people it would reach, and encouraged me to talk about my book and my experiences.

I was excited as I hung up the phone. Why should I even pray? A door this large just *had* to be the will of God. But when I prayed, He showed me that it would result in little increase for the Kingdom. I prayed more, still anxious to go. He showed me a picture of my hands being tied. I knew that meant I would not have freedom to obey the Holy Spirit.

At first I was disappointed and almost angry at God. Then I rejoiced because it was obvious that the Lord was not sending me, and that He was sparing me from the monumental effort of traveling a great distance and putting my nervous system through the whole ordeal. God is smart. I do not know why there would have been little fruit. It is not my business. It does not even matter. The issue is that when God says no, He has something better. He knows how best to utilize what He has deposited in each of us and how to make us the most effective.

On the other hand, I have received invitations to small gatherings that outwardly have seemed unappealing, but the Lord has said yes. When I accept, inevitably the Lord does wonderful things and lives are marvelously changed, confirming that going was in the perfect will of God.

If we live by the natural mind and outward appearances, we rob ourselves of experiencing the potential blessing God has in store. What looks good to our eyes may not look good at all through God's eyes. God sees the end from the beginning. He knows whose hearts are prepared and whose are not. I love God's words to Samuel: "For the LORD does not see as man sees; for man looks at the outward appearance, but the LORD looks at the heart" (1 Samuel 16:7). We need to believe that God simply sees from a far better viewpoint than we do. It pays to inquire of Him.

We can inquire of God anytime, and we can always expect to hear. In the next chapter, I want to talk about the power that is manifested when we hear from heaven.

16

The Power of the Creative Word

Every word God speaks is creative.

He sent His word and healed them.
Psalm 107:20

The meeting was over and several people were standing around chatting. I had just finished preaching in a church located in a small Midwestern town. A man in his late forties stood waiting patiently to talk with me. When the last person walked away, he reached out to shake my hand and asked me if I remembered him. I honestly could not remember ever seeing him before.

"Three years ago," he explained, "you preached one service in my church about thirty miles from here. That night, you had a prophetic word for my wife. You told her that you saw her in the spirit like one who was pregnant."

By now, I was beginning to recall the incident.

"After telling her what you were seeing," he continued, "you said that this meant she was spiritually pregnant and that God was making her more fruitful for the Kingdom of God."

Then he told me the remainder of the amazing story. "Three weeks after you were at our church, we discovered that my wife was pregnant!"

While telling me this, he was holding his little two-year-old daughter in his arms. The more he talked, the more I marveled. At the time the word came forth for his wife, she and her husband were both in their mid-forties and had never had children naturally. It was medically impossible. They did have two adopted teenage boys.

When the word of knowledge was spoken forth, it had creative power with it. It was exciting to me that although I misinterpreted the word of knowledge by telling her it meant spiritual fruitfulness, God still manifested His word to her. Even though I did not know what I was talking about, God did. His word has creative power! God brought His word and intention to pass, even though my mind was in the way.

Already a Reality

Every word God speaks to us (or through us) is full of creative power. No wonder the devil does not want us to hear the voice of God. This gets even more exciting because as soon as the Holy Spirit speaks, it already exists. Every word God speaks is already a reality. God calls things that are not as though they are (see Romans 4:17). When Gideon was full of fear and was weak and helpless, this word came: "And the Angel of the LORD appeared to him, and said to him, 'The LORD is with you, you mighty man of valor!'" (Judges 6:12).

When God speaks to us, whatever He says is *already* a reality, regardless of what our natural eyes see and our circumstances declare. What we must do is embrace the reality that whatever the Holy Spirit is saying is so—now.

When a doctor tells a woman that she is with child, she has no evidence to show anyone, yet it is a reality at that moment. Several months down the road, she will have the manifestation and evidence for everyone to see. But the baby becomes a reality at the moment of conception, not at the time of delivery. That is why no woman is surprised when she gives birth. The baby has been in existence for months. The delivery is only the evidence and manifestation of what has already been fact.

Likewise, when God speaks to you and me, His word is conceived in us. What we must do is embrace it (not analyze what He says), and then the manifestation will follow. His word to us is *equal* to the manifestation. That is why Jesus marveled at the faith of the centurion who said, "But say the word, and my servant will be healed" (Luke 7:7). The centurion recognized the power of the creative word, declaring, "For I also am a man placed under authority, having soldiers under me. And I say to one, 'Go,' and he goes; and to another, 'Come,' and he comes; and to my servant, 'Do this,' and he does it" (Luke 7:8).

God wants us to see that whatever He says is equal to the manifestation. Children know this principle. They know that if a parent gives a promise, it is equal to experiencing it. That is why children spend so much of the day trying to get a parent to say yes to what they want. Once those words come out of your mouth, your kids know they will experience the promise. Children rejoice when you say yes. Even though the manifestation to the promise you are making may be weeks away, in their innocent and believing minds it is already a reality. Your word (in their eyes) is equal to the manifestation.

God operates on the same principle. If we live to hear His voice and then believe what He says, we will see awesome results. Often when God talks, our circumstances seem contrary to what He has spoken. But that is exactly why God gives us the creative word to stand on. The creative word from His mouth guarantees change.

Pressing In Is Key

The key is to press into God's presence. As Christians, we need to spend more time listening to God than doing anything else. When we do hear the Lord, creative power and life flow through His words.

The devil's strategy is to hinder or discourage us from living in more intimate communion with the Holy Spirit. He hates the creative word of God. Both the devil and religious minds oppose prophecy and all the gifts of the Spirit. The devil knows that God's word to you is creative and will bring forth great fruitfulness.

We must therefore be on guard against negativism, fear, unbelief, worry, discouragement and all forms of distraction. All these things come to clog, abort and choke off the flow of the Holy Spirit to our inner man. No wonder the Bible commands us to praise the Lord at all times. There is no greater weapon against any tactic of the devil. Praising God makes Satan flee. A classic example occurred with Jehoshaphat's army. God commanded singers to go out against their enemies, who wound up slaughtering one another:

> And when he had consulted with the people, he appointed those who should sing to the LORD, and who should praise the beauty of holiness, as they went out before the army and were saying: "Praise the LORD, for His mercy endures forever."

157

Now when they began to sing and to praise, the LORD set ambushes against the people of Ammon, Moab, and Mount Seir, who had come against Judah; and they were defeated.

2 Chronicles 20:21–22

Many Christians pray briefly about a decision and then merely do what seems like common sense, not acquiring the mind of the Lord at all. But God must be sought. "He is a rewarder of those who diligently seek Him" (Hebrews 11:6).

In the parable of the unrighteous judge, Jesus taught the disciples how to pray and not lose heart (see Luke 18:1–6). The temptation when we first pray about something is to lose heart or give up. Thoughts come quickly that God is not interested, and we rationalize that He has more important things to concern Himself with. But God will speak clearly to us if we press into Him. Often, it is necessary to pray until we know our spirit is breaking through.

When praying with someone on the phone, there are times when I can hear the Lord clearly concerning what we are discussing. Then there are other times when I cannot hear the Lord until I get totally quiet and pray in the Spirit for a while. Getting off alone quietly and "pressing into" prayer nearly always gets results.

We have all had times when God's voice comes easily and other times when we have to press into God to hear. I do not have an answer for why that is the case. But I do know God is faithful to speak to us. He is worth seeking.

Creative Miracles

One time in Wyoming, the word of the Lord came saying He wanted to heal someone who had no sense of smell. A

70-year-old pastor's wife was present who had smelled nothing since she was a child of four. As I recall, something concerning carbon monoxide had destroyed her sense of smell. The church prayed a brief prayer, and she smelled perfume for the first time in 66 years. The following night she testified about how much she was enjoying smelling coffee, toast and brownies. To God be the glory.

While ministering in a small church in Ohio, right at the end of the service the Holy Spirit spoke that He was healing someone of an athlete's foot condition.

Hearing that, the pastor's wife whispered to her husband, "That's for our son."

Their son was fourteen years old and had battled an athlete's foot condition since he was a toddler. They had tried all manner of medications, seeing several doctors over the years, but with no results. The fungus was not only on his toes, but was covering his feet and creeping up his ankles. When that knowledge of healing came forth from the Holy Spirit, no one actually prayed for the boy in that moment, but God brought the creative word to pass all the same. The next morning, to the amazement of the boy and his parents, there was no sign of any fungus or rash. He was totally healed.

A youth pastor's wife in Tennessee was present at a meeting in which the Holy Spirit spoke of God healing someone with a birthmark. Again, no one prayed for anyone specifically in response, but the following morning the young wife approached the mirror to put makeup over the birthmark on her face. To her awe, God had fulfilled His word and the birthmark she had had for twenty-three years was no longer there.

In a similar meeting, a creative word of knowledge came forth that God was healing someone's nostrils. Two people testified about how their nose membranes had been damaged from drug use nearly twenty years before. They testified that their membranes were totally healed following the meeting. One man shared that because of past drug use, he had had no sense of smell for many years. Yet by the following morning, after he accepted and received the word of the Lord about the healing of nostrils, his sense of smell had been restored. He stood up and told us he had previously complained to his doctor that he had no sense of smell. The doctor's reply was that he should not have taken drugs. The Great Physician healed him anyway.

Do Not Abort the Creative Flow

The Bible is full of abortions and near abortions. For example, when Jesus told His disciples to "launch out into the deep and let down your nets for a catch" (Luke 5:4), Peter almost aborted the creative word of God. He made the classic mistake of letting his brain interfere with the Lord's voice. After all, he figured, they had been fishing all night with no result. But then Peter caught himself in the middle of his rationale and said, "Master, we have toiled all night and caught nothing; *nevertheless at Your word* I will let down the net" (verse 5, emphasis added). As a result, so many fish filled the net that it was breaking, and they had to call their partners to help.

Naaman the Syrian almost aborted his miracle. When the messenger of the prophet told him, "Go and wash in the Jordan seven times, and your flesh shall be restored to you, and you shall be clean" (2 Kings 5:10), he was angry because a miracle would happen differently than he thought. But his servants appealed to him to obey (rather than aborting the miracle) and he was healed (see verses 11–19).

King Joash aborted part of his destiny, because when Elisha told him to strike the ground with the arrows, he only struck it three times. "And the man of God was angry with him, and said, 'You should have struck five or six times; then you would have struck Syria till you had destroyed it! But now you will strike Syria only three times'" (2 Kings 13:19).

The most troublesome enemy of the creative flow, other than the devil, is our analytical mind. God's commands do not always seem reasonable to us, but His commands always bear fruit if they are obeyed.

In the preceding chapters, we have talked about so many ways we can hear from God and so many things that can affect our hearing—things such as coming to His throne boldly, living with expectation, keeping it simple, looking beyond the spectacular, finding our spiritual equilibrium, inquiring in His temple and recognizing the power of His creative word. In the next and final chapter, I want to conclude by giving you something I think will really help you put into practice everything we have talked about. I want to give you a dozen practical guidelines on how to hear God for yourself.

17

Practical Guidelines for Hearing from God

Normal Christianity involves hearing and knowing God's voice.

> However, when He, the Spirit of truth, has come, He will guide you into all truth; for He will not speak in His own authority, but whatever He hears He will speak; and He will tell you things to come.
>
> John 16:13

Waiting on the Lord is hard on the flesh, and it seems as though we all have to go through those times. After resigning the pastorate, I took some speaking engagements, but my mind was continually occupied with figuring out where to relocate. Many days I would visit the post office, hoping and believing there would be some type of invitation for the next step in ministry.

Over the next several months, the Lord spoke various things to me. More than once, He spoke the name "Dixie." I also had a "knowing" during those months that we were being sent to the southeastern United States. One time the Lord spoke "Appalachia." Another time He spoke "six hundred miles." I kept a record of everything the Lord said over those months. The end result was that we ended up living at the base of the Appalachians, and it was almost exactly six hundred miles from our Texas home to our Alabama home. It was not until later, after we moved, that I pulled up to a stoplight one morning and saw that the license plate on the car in front of me read "Heart of Dixie." Looking back, everything the Lord spoke came to pass accurately. It was exciting the way the Lord revealed His will.

Movement Is Key

It is impossible to guide a parked car. You cannot do it. Yet when a car is moving, you can guide it with one finger on the wheel. The key to guidance is movement. When we move toward God, we begin to recognize His mentoring hand. The key is to start moving, and then more direction will come. Sometimes we wait, wanting a thunderbolt from the sky. But as we move, the heavenly Guide gets involved with us.

Before we knew exactly where the Lord wanted us to relocate, we got moving. Not knowing what else to do at the time, we decided to step out in faith and spy out the land, driving to the southeastern part of the United States. We stopped in Birmingham, Alabama, for lunch and had every intention of driving on to Georgia.

As we were getting up from the table in a cafeteria, I stated, "We'll look around Birmingham a little, and then we'll drive on over to Georgia. . . ."

I could not even finish my sentence because as I spoke the words, "We'll look around Birmingham," the Holy Spirit came powerfully over me. Instantly, I knew beyond a shadow of a doubt that this was the city where God was telling us to relocate. Numerous things happened in the following days as the Lord confirmed this, including the opening of an impossible door for the children to attend a Christian school. It all came about because we got on the move, which was key to our receiving guidance.

Guidelines to Help You Hear

Below are a number of guidelines that will help you when you are getting on the move, seeking the Lord and desiring to hear His voice. I may have mentioned some of these already in the previous pages, but reviewing is good.

1. Avoid Distractions

An overactive mind will always be our greatest obstacle in hearing the Holy Spirit. When you need to hear the Lord on a certain subject, the best thing to do is remove yourself from distractions that will cause your mind to wander, such as the refrigerator, a ringing phone, the television or a magazine lying too handy.

When we begin to seek the Lord, it never ceases to amaze me how quickly our mind is flooded with ideas of other things to do. These ideas come with great urgency. Obviously, the devil will do *anything* to distract us from spending time with God. Thoughts of washing the car, cleaning out a closet and other insignificant activities are not uncommon choices that come to mind. Knowing the devil is that worried about my spending time with God actually adds excitement to my praying.

If we put God first and give Him time in prayer, He redeems our time for the rest of the day. Along with making an appointment or setting a specific time to pray, it is good to have a specific place to pray. This conditions your spirit to be in more of a posture to receive from God.

If I am home alone, sometimes it helps to turn the lights down so that I avoid becoming distracted by looking around the room. If I am praying with a group of people, however, the voice of the Lord always seems to come very clearly, probably because we all are focused on Him.

2. Show the Holy Spirit Respect

Treat the Holy Spirit like the person He really is. Reverence Him. No one likes being used, including God. Approach Him first with thanksgiving and praise (see Psalm 100). We should always take time to thank Him specifically for answered prayer and for His goodness. God cannot resist a thankful heart. I personally believe that the lack of gratitude hinders us from hearing the Lord. Yet some Christians seem to carry around an attitude that says, "What has God done for me lately?"

3. Pray for the Increase of the Kingdom

Pray first for the increase of God's Kingdom. Ask the Holy Spirit what is on *His* mind. Pray in the Spirit and pray in English (or your native language).

Wait on God to speak. As you pray concerning Kingdom needs, He will put words in your mouth. You will hear yourself praying prophetically, and your words will express the will of God specifically in regard to what you are praying.

Before I learned to pray first for the increase of the Kingdom, I would begin with listing my needs before God. It was almost like a small child droning over a catalog and telling Dad, "I would sure like this, and this, and this."

As God dealt with me, it was as if I could hear Him saying "boring, boring, boring" regarding my self-centered prayers. We would do well to remember Matthew 6:33: "But seek first the kingdom of God and His righteousness, and all these things shall be added to you."

If you want to bless people, you ask about their needs. Nothing is more flattering than when you show interest in someone. If you ask grandparents about their children or grandchildren, they immediately pull pictures out of their billfold, enthralled that you asked. God is the same way. Ask Him about His children. Let Him take out His "billfold" and show you their needs. Ask Him who is on His mind and who needs prayer that day.

After praying for Kingdom needs, bring up your needs and questions. That way, you will not experience the dryness and struggle that was present when you tried praying only for yourself.

4. Pray about One Thing at a Time

As I mentioned previously, most people mistakenly ask God for wisdom and direction concerning several subjects at a time. Not praying specifically leads to confusion, because when the Holy Spirit speaks to you through a picture, words or in some other manner as you pray, it is difficult to know which subject He is addressing if you have been bringing up multiple subjects.

It is of utmost importance to ask God only *one* question at a time and then take time to listen for a few minutes. Record whatever impression you feel in reply—what you hear or see by the Spirit—before moving on to another question you want to ask the Lord. God is very practical, so in order for you to understand what He is saying, you must ask specifically. Then when He does speak, you will know precisely what subject He is addressing.

For example, if you are in a situation where you have three job offers, you obviously want to know from the Lord which one is best for you. Pray about each one specifically, and write down what you hear or see. After praying this way, it will become obvious which job the Lord is most strongly giving you direction about.

Many believers do not realize that this type of conversation with the Holy Spirit is possible, so they labor on in prayer for direction on various things—asking God to help them meet the house payment, asking Him to show them a new job or to guide them regarding an offer on something—all in one breath. This leaves them unfulfilled, frustrated and even confused.

God wants to talk to you concerning each individual area you pray about. That is why it is so important to pray specifically about one thing at a time if you are asking for His direction.

5. Pray with Expectation

Many people have been taught to pray in generalities by presenting God with a long list of needs. In fact, we often conclude that the longer our list, the more satisfied we will be that we have pleased God. This type of prayer is okay when interceding for the needs of various people, but not when seeking God for specific guidance.

Be convinced that God *is* going to talk to you. Remember that prayer is a two-way conversation. In order to hear from God, you need to know that He will talk to you *right then and there* as you are praying. Without expectation and a belief that you will hear an answer, why pray?

Yes, a Christian can actually sit down and pray about a decision and hear the Holy Spirit give an answer in the following few minutes. This kind of news seems almost too good to be true, but it is true.

6. Do Not Try to Persuade God to Change His Mind

This can be a hard lesson to learn. Even though we do not like to admit it, sometimes our mind is more made up than we realize, and we go back again and again to the Lord to obtain the answer we desire. Whether consciously or subconsciously, the human will is strong and determined. The difficulty is that we want the Lord to confirm what we want more than we want what He wants.

Of course, this becomes a problem mostly when we are praying about something we really want to do. Our emotions are riding high, and frankly, many times they simply override the will of the Spirit. Emotions are part of the soul. The power of the soul can be so convincing that we deceive ourselves into thinking we have the mind of the Spirit. God will show us the difference.

Impulsive people have the most difficulty in hearing from God, because they are accustomed to making decisions based on impulse and their initial excitement. It seems hardest for these people to submit their adrenaline flow to the Holy Spirit and become quiet enough to listen. But impulsive people usually get burned by making hasty decisions based on temporary emotions.

The other extreme, however, is being fearful of making a decision. The Lord spoke to me once that the root of indecision is pride. Some will not make a decision for fear of making the wrong decision and hurting their pride.

There are also some decisions that God leaves totally up to us. In answer to our prayer, God says, "What do you want to do?" But He will always give us wisdom if we ask.

7. Do Not Demand That God Be Sensational

Some believe anything God does will be sensational and spectacular, as we talked about in chapter 13. This kind of thinking is contrary to fellowship and intimacy with the Holy Spirit. In reality, when the Holy Spirit speaks to us, it can almost be described as slight or subtle. His gentle promptings, quiet nudges and silent illuminations never come with force. We must reach out for them, and accept and embrace them.

The Holy Spirit is a gentleman. Many times when He speaks to us, it will be quiet—so quiet that the natural mind wants to dismiss it. We have to *train* ourselves to recognize and trust the still, small voice. Take time to fellowship with the Holy Spirit. "The grace of the Lord Jesus Christ, and the love of God, and the communion [fellowship] of the Holy Spirit be with you all" (2 Corinthians 13:14).

8. Be Neutral—No Emotions

One of the most difficult things to do is pray about something when you are emotionally involved. When we want to do something badly enough, it is hard to pray objectively, with an open mind. And when we do pray, it is easy to convince ourselves that we are hearing the Lord say yes to our inquiry.

One time Elisha had to call for a musician when he needed a word from God, because his emotions (of displeasure) were involved:

> And Elisha said, "As the LORD of hosts lives, before whom I stand, surely were it not that I regard the presence of Jehoshaphat king of Judah, I would not look at you, nor see you. But now bring me a musician."

Then it happened, when the musician played, that the hand of the LORD came upon him. And he said, "Thus says the LORD: 'Make this valley full of ditches.'"

2 Kings 3:14–16

It is easier for some people to shift their emotions into neutral when asking the Lord for His will and wisdom. They can compartmentalize their emotions, set aside what they want and be totally open to what God wants. But quite frankly, many in the Body of Christ simply hear their emotions when they pray and are unable to discern the difference between the enthusiasm of their feelings and the mind of the Spirit. When it comes to making a decision, instead of hearing God, most people weigh the pros and cons, the advantages and disadvantages, and make their decision based on human reasoning and not in obedience to a nod from the Holy Spirit.

Other times, people miss the Lord simply because they cannot say no. The fear of people holds them in such bondage that they submit to someone's request because they cannot pick up the phone and say, "I'm sorry, but God isn't leading me to do that."

Often, when counseling people concerning a decision, we have to remind them that the bottom line is this: The mind of the Lord is either yes or no. Weighing all the options is not necessarily wrong, but ultimately, either it *is* the mind of the Lord, or it *is not*.

9. Trust Your First Impressions

Simply through the reasoning process, the mind of a person is quick to defile what the mind of the Holy Spirit has spoken. When you seek God for His direction, it is often the first impression you have that is the most accurate, even though it may seem slight. If you discount that first impression, soon your mind begins to analyze the situation and to bring forth pros and cons, and then confusion sets in.

It is good to go back and recall the first impression you had when you began to pray. As James 1:5 says, "If any of you lacks wisdom, let him ask of God, who gives to all liberally and without reproach, and it will be given to him."

10. Do Not Take Yourself Too Seriously

Do not take yourself too seriously . . . no one else does! God is in control of our lives. He is in the management department. As a young Christian, I never laughed. There was little joy. I was trying to be spiritual. But in my trying, I only became religious.

At my ordination, a minister prayed over me, then prophesied, "My son, the Lord has given you a ministry of joy . . ."

That joy has increased more and more in me. Meetings simply are fun now. Life is more fun.

There is something about trying too hard that constricts the flow of the Holy Spirit. The harder *you* try, the less room there is for *God* to get through. Laugh at yourself. You will hear God more clearly. Do not take yourself so seriously, but *do* take God seriously. Fervently seek Him. Fervently love Him. Then relax.

11. Do Not Be a Perfectionist

The bondage of perfectionism robs us of enjoying God and constricts us from hearing clearly. Much of the teaching from various Christian circles implies that we must not fail God in anything. While it is true that we do not want to fail

God intentionally, we have to realize that He leaves room for "missing" His voice. It is in exercising our listening to God where the Holy Spirit will say, "Try again."

Some of God's choicest servants made horrible blunders. Even when we sincerely intend to obey, there will be times when we just do not hear, or we misinterpret what we hear. But praise God, there is freedom to fail in the Kingdom of God—but not freedom to be irresponsible. If you miss it . . . admit it.

Most Christians can recall times when the Lord was telling them to do something and they ignored the voice—only to find out later that in ignoring the voice, they missed a wonderful opportunity. But as long as we are attempting to pay attention to God and listen to the Holy Spirit, there is no guilt, and there are no feelings of failure or condemnation (see Romans 8:1).

Perfectionism is an incredible bondage. Perfectionists usually are miserable people. Many come from religious backgrounds that advocate and even dictate perfectionism. It is out of this context that, trying so hard never to miss God on anything, we often miss Him completely.

Religious perfectionism misses the essence of the message of the Gospel. The Gospel is good news. The good news is that we have been called into relationship with God, *not* into a religious performance.

12. Get to Know God More Intimately

God's purpose is for us to grow in our relationship and intimacy with Him. Be careful not to separate your relationship with God from the petitions and wisdom you seek from Him, using Him as a vending machine to get what you are asking for.

All of life flows out of our relationship with Him. He wants our fellowship with Him enhanced on a daily basis.

He can easily redeem our mistakes—what He wants is our heart. Do not seek a formula. Seek Him.

It is easy to fall in the trap of working *for* God instead of working *with* God. We can fool ourselves into doing the works of God without having a heart toward God Himself. Even though we are actively involved in ministry, it is possible to be living in a "distant" relationship with God and thereby not be hearing the proceeding word. The way to guard against that is by living with a passion to know Him more and more intimately.

Keep Your Heart Pliable

God's word to the children of Israel was always an exhortation to hear His voice, combined with a warning not to harden their hearts. We can all be guilty of having a hard heart, so His word in Psalm 95:7–8 is as applicable to us today as it was when it came to the children of Israel: "Today, if you will hear His voice: 'Do not harden your hearts as in the rebellion.'"

It is important to realize that going to church is no guarantee that people will not harden their hearts. Church can be a great place to fall into a formulaic Christianity and hide from an intimate relationship with God. "The backslider in heart will be filled with his own ways, but a good man will be satisfied from above" (Proverbs 14:14). The bottom line is, *do we really want to hear?*

We all have a tendency to run from God at times. In fact, if we are honest, there are times when we are not sure we want to hear the Lord—especially if He is bringing correction. We also honestly have to admit that, many times, we do not want to pray about a decision because we are afraid the Lord might say no. Many sincere ministers live this way, stiff-arming the

Holy Spirit as they conduct the work of the ministry. The only way we can escape His voice is to harden our hearts so that His tugging does not make us so uncomfortable.

We must choose not to harden our hearts, and one of the ways we do that is by keeping our ears open and by listening for the many ways that He can and does speak to us every day. It is key to allow the Holy Spirit to keep the soil of our hearts pliable and stirred at all times. In that sense, "give us this day our daily bread" takes on a meaning beyond being fed naturally. If we are not hearing that proceeding word of "fresh bread" from heaven, our hearts can easily crust over and become callused, just like soil that has had no rain. As Christians, we are meant to hear God as a perpetual, daily occurrence.

Let me give one final caution as we come to the end of these pages: Keep your heart pliable and soft toward God so that you can hear His voice. Be listening for the still, small voice of God that will guide you, direct you and give you insight and wisdom when you need it. It may come through His Word, the Bible. It may come through the proceeding word or through His thoughts in your mind. It may come through words of knowledge or through His words dropped into your spirit. He may speak to your heart through pictures, visions or dreams. He may speak by giving you a sense of peace (or a lack of peace). You may hear Him through an inner witness or through your conscience. You may hear Him in some other way I have not covered in these pages. But you will hear Him, if you are listening.

Come boldly to God's throne and ask Him to speak to you. Then live with expectation and faith that He will do so. You can hear the voice of God!

Steve Sampson is a gifted writer and effective minister who provides the Body of Christ with thought-provoking insights about the ministry of the Holy Spirit. His unique wit, combined with candor and transparency, refreshes the soul of the hearer.

Through the prophetic gifts of the Holy Spirit, Steve has ministered in many countries for decades by speaking personal vision, hope and expectation into the lives of thousands. Demonstrating how the Holy Spirit speaks to people, he has been a source of encouragement for others who seek to experience the power and fullness of life in the Spirit.

You can contact Steve about ministry events and available teaching resources at:

Steve Sampson Ministries
P.O. Box 36324
Birmingham, AL 35236
www.stevesampson.com

More from Steve Sampson

In this eye-opening classic, Steve Sampson shows you how to protect yourself and, if necessary, break free from the Jezebel spirit—a demonic spirit of control. Discover the signs of a Jezebel spirit, its strategies of destruction and how to bring it under the power of the Holy Spirit. This biblical guide is the definitive resource for anyone needing to confront this demonic entity.

Confronting Jezebel

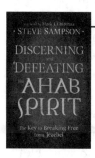

Using sound biblical teaching and real-life illustrations, Steve Sampson reveals how to discern and defeat the spirit of Ahab, Jezebel's ancient ally. It is possible to be assertive in a godly way, and this book will help believers trapped in passivity due to the controlling influence of the Jezebel spirit to claim their freedom and become a positive force for change.

Discerning and Defeating the Ahab Spirit

 **Chosen**

 Stay up-to-date on your favorite books and authors with our free e-newsletters. Sign up today at chosenbooks.com.

 Find us on Facebook. facebook.com/chosenbooks

 Follow us on Twitter. @chosenbooks